Vajrasattva Meditation

Vajrasattva Meditation

An Illustrated Guide

Khenpo Yeshe Phuntsok

Wisdom Publications · Boston

Wisdom Publications
199 Elm Street
Somerville, MA 02144 USA
www.wisdompubs.org

Library of Congress Cataloging-in-Publication Data

Yeshe Phuntsok, Khenpo, 1971– author.
Vajrasattva meditation : an illustrated guide / Khenpo Yeshe Phuntsok.
pages cm
ISBN 978-1-61429-188-6 — ISBN 978-1-61429-205-0 — ISBN 1-61429-188-8
(pbk. : alk. paper)
1. Tantric Buddhism—Tibet Region—Rituals. 2. Meditation—Tibetan Buddhism.
3. Vajrasattva (Buddhist deity)—Cult—Tibet Region. I. Title.
BQ8920.Y48 2014
294.3′4435—dc23
2014020588

ISBN 978-1-61429-188-6   ebook ISBN 978-161429-205-0

19 18 17 16 15   5 4 3 2 1

English translation by Ke Jiang.
Editorial development of English edition by Lea Groth-Wilson.
Artwork by Zhang Hongying and Cao Liangbo and Winfield Klein.
Cover design by Judith Arisman.
Interior design by Gopa&Ted2, Inc. Set in Cochin LT Std 11.2/15.4.

Please visit www.fscus.org.

CONTENTS

PREFACE

Namo Guru Vajrasattva!

I F W E E X A M I N E all that we know of human history, it is rare to find a time of happiness and certainty. As human beings, we suffer from what we *cannot* avoid—from death and old age and the grief of losing our loved ones. More frequently, though, we suffer from what we *do not* avoid. That is, we suffer because we do not refrain from deeply ingrained habits of harmful thoughts, unhelpful speech, and acts driven by our negative emotions.

How often have we wished to let go of all those regrettable actions and painful memories and be more positive, more generous, and more at ease? We understand that our past actions, and the imprints they have left on our psyche, haunt us, making happiness and fulfillment difficult. We search for a spiritual path to alleviate our pain and to fulfill this wish to be free. Yet even when we enter into a spiritual practice, we find we are still weighed down by all our habits and fears, and progress toward contentment, compassion, and wisdom is slow.

Fortunately for us, there are methods on the spiritual path to address our predicament and accelerate our progress. Buddha Samantabhadra said in the Great Perfection tantras that it is at times of strife and degradation that Vajrasattva Buddha is able to widely liberate sentient beings. Given the state of our environment, economy, and politics in this day and age, Vajrasattva purification meditation is the most potent method for removing the cancer that is our painful actions, memories, and habits.

I compiled this book according to many Buddhist scriptures so that practitioners could correctly visualize and properly generate the essential elements for purification. In particular, this book follows the meditational liturgy called *The Precious Wish-Fulfilling Bead: A Vajrasattva Sadhana*, translated and adapted for the present work. This text was a revelation, or *mind terma*, of my root guru, the great khenpo and Dharma king Jigme Phuntsok Rinpoche. Unlike most treasure texts, this one can be practiced even without an empowerment.

Mind termas such as this one appear only rarely and only to those who have already purified their mind to great depths. Such treasure revealers are like buddhas living among us. Jigme Phuntsok Rinpoche was such a presence. I am ever indebted to him, and the more I learn, the more my reverence and gratitude for his teachings increases. A brief presentation of his life and accomplishments can be found in the back of this book.

I originally compiled this book in Chinese when there were already many Chinese Buddhists diligently practicing this liturgy. The number of mantra recitations reported to me by those practitioners was staggering, and the enthusiasm for the practice was undeniable. My goal was to enhance the quality of the practice. To that end, I created this step-by-step guide with pictures for the entire liturgy along with explanations of the process of purification and tips for purifying each of the most serious misdeeds and common nonvirtues. It later became clear that there were no books of this kind in English, despite the plethora of books on tantra and Buddhism in general. To fill this void and to bring this incredibly fast and thorough method for righting past wrongs to more people, I sought to have this book made available in English as well.

My ardent wish is that this book will benefit all who come across it with the means to create greater happiness, peace, harmony, and compassion. May all be auspicious and of great benefit to all beings!

Khenpo Yeshe Phuntsok
Larung Gar Buddhist Institute, 2014

INTRODUCTION

The Tantric Approach

WHILE ALL THE MANY METHODS that the Buddha taught are valid, when it comes to our individual needs, we need the approach that best suits our temperament. Many have found the tantric method well suited to contemporary times. The modern world has many multitaskers, who are not only capable but even addicted to accomplishing more than one thing at a time. For those whose hands, eyes, thought, and speech all seek activity simultaneously, who do not try to be totally immersed in one activity but rather are totally preoccupied with many, the tantric approach makes a lot of sense. With tantra we capitalize on this habit of multitasking. Our hands twirl the 108 beads of the mala rosary. Our eyes may rest on the images of the buddhas we seek to become. Our thoughts visualize and contemplate the image of the buddha we are looking at, bringing it into our space and time. Our vocal chords vibrate with Sanskrit syllables that activate our subtle nervous system. Moreover, with the tantric approach we find buddhas tailored to different needs: for instance, Medicine Buddha for when we are sick, wealth deities for when we are penniless, wrathful deities for when we are overwhelmed by anger or fear.

In this text we focus on the practice of Vajrasattva, the buddha of purification, who diminishes the obscurations and negativity that keep us from receiving the insights of the Buddha. Visualization is central to the tantric approach, and this book helps refine our vision of the deity. Vajrasattva is generally white in color. Royal and majestic, he wears a crown, silks, and jewels. He sits cross-legged on a grand lotus throne. Resplendent with light, like a thousand suns, his body is present, but there is nothing solid or opaque about him; he is not a human with bone and tissue. His form is like a rainbow—present and clear, but ungraspable. He radiates compassion and wisdom. The heart of this book explains and shows in great detail his form and attributes.

This book is for Buddhist practitioners, particularly those who have had an introduction to the Vajrasattva practice from a qualified teacher and are looking to perform a *sadhana*, or meditational liturgy, of Vajrasattva. Normally a practitioner needs an empowerment or initiation to visualize tantric deities. The unique quality of the sadhana in this book is that it does not require such an empowerment. Nonetheless, a Vajrasattva initiation would increase the strength of the practitioner's connection and commitment.

In Vajrasattva practice, meditators typically visualize Vajrasattva and his purifying power entering and washing through them in the form of white nectar while they recite a hundred-syllable mantra. This light clears away the accumulation of negative karma and creates a foundation for the path to enlightenment. Eventually, through this purifying light, they may become indivisible from Vajrasattva himself, which is to say, fully enlightened. In the particular liturgy illustrated in this book, the *Wish-Fulfilling Precious Bead* (*Rdo rje sems dpa'i sgrub thabs tsinta ma ni*), the nature of Vajrasattva is visualized as one's root guru, so it combines guru yoga with purification practice. Its name indicates that it is as powerful as a magic wish-granting jewel, since it is the door to peerless happiness.

To derive the greatest benefit from this book, it is important to understand two things: the idea of purification and the nature of Vajrasattva. By understanding the concept, need, and approach of purification, our motivation and enthusiasm for it will be correctly developed. By appreciating the qualities and nature of Vajrasattva, our faith and trust in this method will deepen. Without having trust in the method or a reason for applying it, this book will remain for us only pictures and letters. Then, even if we were to recite the prayers and mantras a million times, while this would be more virtuous than doing nothing at all, it would be like going to the hospital with cancer and only seeing a receptionist. To this end, we begin by exploring why we need purification, how it works, who Vajrasattva is, and why the practice of Vajrasattva is so powerful.

Why We Need Purification

The main obstacles that prevent all the extraordinary experiences and
realizations of the profound path from arising are negative actions,
obscurations, and habitual tendencies. Just as it is important to clean
the surface of a mirror if forms are to be reflected in it, so too it is
important to eliminate our obscurations so that realization can appear
like a reflection in the mirror of the Ground of All. The Buddha
taught countless methods of purification for this purpose,
but the best of them all is meditation and recitation
related to the teacher as Vajrasattva.[1]

—PATRUL RINPOCHE (1808–87)

A S UNENLIGHTENED BEINGS, we are obscured. We are obscured
by our past and we are obscured by our habits; we are obscured
by our emotions and we are obscured by our thoughts. We experience the world through the filter of our five senses and our mind.
Because it appears to us that we have a body and mind that we seem
to control most of the time, we fall into the mistaken, but nearly
innate, belief that we are somehow separate, isolated individuals
who are different from all the things beyond our control, like the
grass, the mountains, and other beings. While this belief is logical
from the relative perspective of everyday life, it is nonetheless what
leads us into the depths of suffering.

Why does the belief in an independent self and phenomena lead us into suffering? Since this belief is false, it is an unsound basis for action. Essentially, without this misperception of a substantive self, we would cling to nothing. Without this perception of a concrete and uncontrollable world, we would fear nothing. Without this primal ignorance of "me" and "not-me" or the resultant attachment and aversion, there would be no cause or condition for deluded thoughts, words, and actions. Without these, there is no karma, let alone a means or basis for positive and negative. Without karma there would be nothing to keep us trapped life after life experiencing birth, old age, sickness, and death.

More to the point, the many countless actions we have committed since beginningless time have been largely negative actions — not negative in the eyes of society perhaps but negative in the sense of keeping us trapped in *samsara*, the suffering cycle of rebirths. At any time these unwholesome acts can drag us into the abyss of the lower realms and painful experiences. We cannot get rid of the seeds of negative karma without a method. The best method is that of the undeceiving Buddha Vajrasattva.

THE PROBLEM OF KARMA

How does karma trap us in cyclic existence? Because every action, word, or thought that originates from our consciousness leaves an imprint of that act, word, or thought in our base consciousness, our mental continuum. These imprints are like seeds. They condition the future acts, words, and experiences that we will reap in this and future lives. Moreover these imprints stain our mindstreams, making it difficult to realize our true nature, not to mention making us more likely to repeat the same problematic behaviors.

In other words, whenever we do, say, or think something negative against someone, it leaves an imprint that we will experience later as an unpleasant result. This is like polluting the source of a river—the water downstream becomes polluted as well. When we do, say, or think something positive, however, as in something that benefits others, this leaves a positive imprint that will later result in a pleasant circumstance or experience, such as another opportunity to do something beneficial. This positive imprint is like pumping fresh water back into the river—the bottom of the water is again easier to see. Clarity returns to the mind.

We can find evidence of the mechanics of karma every day. Constantly, our experience is changed and conditioned by all our thoughts, speech, and actions. When we do something kind, we generally feel positive about ourselves, and others respond kindly to us as well. On the other hand, when we do something less than kind, usually we do so because we are not happy in some way. Acting out our dissatisfaction may gratify us temporarily, but this passes into the unpleasant result of guilt from within or of retribution from others.

That negative imprints bring unpleasant results is problematic enough, but what keeps us truly mired in samsara is that these imprints ferment. Each day that goes by without purifying multiplies the magnitude of the negative act. Say we step on someone's toe today; later it could ferment into the karmic result of losing a limb!

Even if we lead a saintly life and never have a selfish thought, let alone cause even a flea any discomfort, we cannot be certain of the imprinted negative actions, words, and thoughts that we may have committed in previous lives that are still fermenting and waiting for the opportune moment to erupt into our present or future experience. Virtue alone does not guarantee us a peaceful ride to enlightenment. What virtuous behavior does guarantee is that we are not further planting in our mental continuum the seeds of future suffering. Even if it is not the entire solution to being free of suffering, it is still very beneficial. But only through purification and consistently practicing methods such as Vajrasattva can we completely remove the seeds and imprints of karma that keep us trapped in suffering life after life.

EMOTIONAL OBSCURATION

Generally speaking, what leads us to accumulate negative karma is the obscuration fueled by afflictive emotions. This is the obscuration that posits a truly existent self, which catapults us into a plethora of needs, wants, preoccupations, and defenses that arise as the various emotions. So we get angry, envious, or lustful, we overvalue or undervalue ourselves, or we end up in a sort of dull confusion. We seek fame, comfort, and gain, or we try to avoid pain, anonymity, and loss. In all these ways, we veil our innate goodness and fall into emotional obscuration.

The five major afflictive emotions of anger, jealousy, desire, pride, and ignorance, not to mention all the minor variations thereof, are never innocent; they do not bring ultimate benefit to anyone. Their very nature is to destroy our peace of mind as well as the peace of mind of all those that they come in contact with. Even righteous anger and the unquenchable thirst for truth or peace are unsettling and thus obscure the true nature of the mind. These emotions are like turbulence in water, which swirls up mud and silt, obscuring the clearness of the water itself. Their mere presence in our mind is a nonvirtue, not just because they unsettle our minds and nervous systems, but also because they rarely stay only as mental activities. Before we can stop them, they have become harmful words or violent actions, and we have increased our karmic burden that much more.

COGNITIVE OBSCURATIONS

Unlike the intensity and obviousness of the emotions, cognitive obscurations are subtle and difficult to uncover. This is because cognitive obscurations proliferate from our inability to penetrate the mistaken notion of a concrete and discrete self and other, or to comprehend phenomena without language and concept. In particular it is the cognitive veil that posits a truly existent world. Any thought that is underpinned with subject, object, or action is laced with this obscuration. These are like the ripples on a body of water that reflect light and make it difficult to see through to the bottom of the water. While this seems like a philosophical obscuration, it is actually quite basic and one of the last to be removed before complete enlightenment.

Vajrasattva practice addresses even this most subtle obscuration. In the moment when the visualization dissolves and we are resting in the awareness of emptiness, in what is called the dissolution phase, we are in fact removing the veiling effects of this obscuration. In that moment of clear dissolution, even if it is only for a fraction of a second, our mind is resting in a state free from all these cognitive obscurations, free from concepts of self and other, free from mental ripples of any kind. To hold this awareness for even a moment profoundly diminishes this obscuration.

HABITUAL TENDENCIES

Another major problem with karmic imprints, besides their fermentation and obscuration of the mind, is that they become habitual, like well-worn grooves in our consciousness. We have all had the experience at some point of an action becoming easier through repetition, whether learning to play an instrument or simply snapping our fingers. The first time we tried, it was almost impossible, but it got easier with each attempt, and after many tries it became second nature, and we no longer had to consciously think about how to do it. The same is unfortunately true of negative thinking, speaking, and acting. We do not remember the first time in our many lives that we acted out of anger or lust. These reactions long ago became grooves that we deepened and made second nature with each new anger and desire. Sometimes these grooves are great gorges with all the times we have repeated the same action or reaction. To bring ourselves out of these chasms of habitual patterns is like scaling Mount Everest. Often it is said that habitual tendencies are the most difficult to overcome, even more than intellectual or emotional obscurations, because they arise so automatically and often unconsciously.

Jigme Phuntsok Rinpoche often said, "Without practicing persistently, we cannot eradicate the habitual tendencies accumulated since beginningless time nor maintain or stabilize the wisdom that we attained earlier. Therefore we should spare no efforts in doing all virtuous deeds and listening, contemplating, and meditating on the Dharma." Fortunately, Vajrasattva practice is like a great bird that picks us out of the canyons of our negative patterns. He is our guide that brings us back on the plains, giving us the possibility to make new grooves, this time positive ones. Ultimately the practice will free us entirely from canyons and plains, positive and negative, cognitive and emotional obscurations, imprints and grooves, self and other, and finally, even from the practice itself.

How Purification Works

Through the practice of Vajrasattva and the process of purification, we are acknowledging that we have knowingly and unknowingly done, said, and thought many things that were not beneficial and were often quite harmful. In this acknowledgment, we are implicitly and explicitly confessing with deep remorse any and all harm that we have brought into the many lives that we have lived and impacted. This regret gives us the resolve to avoid further imprinting our consciousness with negativity. When we go through this process in the presence of Vajrasattva, it is like standing before a compassionate tribunal that has the power to accept our sincere confession and remove our debt.

Unless we can rest totally and completely in the absolute nature of mind, it would be a misunderstanding to think that a mere good confession would free us from karma. If it could, then karma would not be the infallible principle guiding all existence that it is. There is no way to get around the fact that all causes have a result. When we talk about purifying and washing away misdeeds, this does not mean that causes already imprinted will bear no results at all. That is possible only for those of the highest capacity who can rest totally in the awareness of emptiness at all times.

For the majority of us who cannot maintain this awareness, we will still experience some result from our previously imprinted karma. Purification, however, can mitigate the experience of those results. This means that rather than experiencing the results as manifold times worse in their fermented form, we will experience the results in the gentlest possible manner. Then, at some point in our process of purification, these karmic results will in effect become the blessings that advance us along the path to complete enlightenment.

There is a story of the Buddha where he is walking through a garden and steps on a thorn. Normally the Buddha's feet walk so lightly on the earth that they cannot possibly harm any insects, let alone be pricked by a thorn. So when the Buddha gets hurt, his disciples are horrified and in disbelief. Ananda, the Buddha's faithful servant, asks the Buddha how this possibly could have happened. The Buddha responds that one time, before he was the Buddha, he stepped on an ant without realizing it. This thorn was the result of that. The Buddha manifested this for our benefit, to remind us that all causes have results, no matter how far along the path we may think we are. The Buddha demonstrated something else in this story, too. He did not yelp, curse, cry, or bemoan his fate when his foot was bleeding from the thorn. His bleeding foot was not experienced, we are led to understand, any differently from his foot not bleeding from a thorn. That was the second teaching.

The point is that purification does not eliminate karmic results altogether; it minimizes results and transforms our experience of those results. Without purification, the result of stepping on an ant, even accidentally, could ferment into death under the wheels of a truck, thus catapulting us into another life, perhaps in the lowest realms. Through purification the effect is minimized to something quite insignificant that even becomes a teaching, a beneficial act, for others. Even though eventually we, like the Buddha, will come to experience the results of our actions, our ability to turn good and bad circumstances into simple, neutral events depends on purification.

By generating the visualization of Vajrasattva and then really feeling that all our negative emotions and the actions and misdeeds that have arisen out of them are being washed away by the stream of nectar descending from Vajrasattva's limitless compassion for us, we really can eliminate the emotional obscurations as well as diminish the karmic imprints and their ripening results from our mindstream. So although we cannot wash away the results of our actions per se, we can purify our attachment and aversions to those results and minimize their severity. When we do this, all experiences, even obstacles, become footsteps on the path to total liberation; difficulties turn into blessings. Sooner or later, because of Vajrasattva and his hundred-syllable mantra, all circumstances become streams of purification and deepen our experience of pure awareness, which in essence is as though the negative karma had been completely eliminated.

Even when we are not engaged in Vajrasattva practice, if we can stay aware of our body, speech, and mind and avoid further negative karmic imprints, we will enhance our lives and our practice tremendously, not to mention the lives of all those we come into contact with.

PURIFICATION THROUGH THE FOUR OPPONENT POWERS

To maximize the potency of Vajrasattva practice, we rely on what are called the *four opponent powers*: reliance, regret, resolve, and the remedy. We cultivate the power of *reliance* through taking refuge and generating bodhichitta, the altruistic thought of awakening. We develop the power of *regret* through examining our misdeeds and then confessing them sincerely. We generate the power of *resolve* by vowing to abstain from misdeeds. Then we develop the power of the actual *remedy* through reciting the hundred-syllable mantra. Finally, we increase the merit of purification through dedicating it to the enlightenment of all sentient beings.

The power of reliance

We develop the power of reliance through an inner cause and outer conditions. The inner cause is the mind of refuge and *bodhichitta*, the wish to become a buddha in order to free all beings. The outer condition is the aspiration and vow of Vajrasattva, which makes him an infallible source of refuge. First we reflect on the good qualities of Vajrasattva to generate supreme faith. This leads us to taking refuge in him with a single-pointed mind. Second, we reflect on the suffering of sentient beings in the six realms. From this we feel greater compassion and aspire to purify their negative karma, resulting in our generating bodhichitta. Without taking refuge, it is not a Buddhist practice; without generating bodhichitta, it is not a Mahayana practice. Therefore it is important to give proper emphasis to taking refuge and generating bodhichitta before we begin the practice. We will explore refuge and bodhichitta more fully in the explanation of the main practice.

The power of regret

We know that cancer can spread and metastasize to other parts of the body if we do not treat it. In order to catch cancer in its earliest and easiest-to-treat stage, we get regular and thorough physical exams. If cancer is found, we rely on a doctor to remove it, take our medicine, and try to eradicate the possible causes and carcinogens. Only in this way can the cancer eventually be cured.

Similarly, the imprint of negative karma is like a cancer in our mental continuum, causing harm to our body, speech, or mind. If we do not check for it and counteract it regularly, the seeds of negative karma will mature, and then even the Buddha will not be able to stop it. Therefore it is very important to track down negative karma as early as possible, before it has the chance to mature, and purify it immediately.

How do we track down our negative karma? We call to mind and reflect on the situations where we have committed negative deeds.

After remembering them, we regret them thoroughly in our hearts, confess them with our words, and show respect through bowing in front of Vajrasattva without hiding anything. If our feeling of regret is deep and sincere, then we possess the power of regret.

We should investigate as thoroughly as possible and examine all negative actions we have committed in one category, such as the nonvirtue of killing. Then we continue reflecting in other categories, such as lying or wrong view. Finally, we confess each of them deeply from our hearts. To aid this process, the end of this book includes contemplations on each of the major categories of nonvirtue. Even if we do not find many negative actions in a given category in this life, that does not mean that we did not commit them in previous lives. We can still cultivate the power of regret for actions we no longer remember or we did unknowingly. In this way, the negative karma can be mitigated, just as dust scatters with a puff of air.

The power of resolve

The power of resolve is to vow with a clear visualization: "From now on, even if my life is endangered, I will never again commit this negative action." The key here is to cultivate a sincere feeling to never do that negative action again. Only in this way can the fermentation of that negative karma be stopped. Otherwise, your confession is just nonsense.

The power of the remedy

The power of the remedy, the actual antidote in this practice, is to recite the hundred-syllable mantra of Vajrasattva. Like the best medicine, this mantra has matchless power to promptly destroy karmic obscurations. The goal here is to believe that the mantra and Buddha Vajrasattva are the same, without any difference, and then to calm your body, speech, and mind and recite the mantra with a focused mind and clear visualization.

Why Vajrasattva Is the Buddha of Purification

B efore he was a buddha, Vajrasattva was a being like us, struggling on the path to awakening. He was what is called a *bodhisattva*, a being who has promised to truly wake up for the sake of all others. Unlike some other bodhisattvas, his path was fraught with obstacles. In one story from the *Collected Intentions of All Buddhas*,[2] Vajrasattva gave teachings that were unsuitably advanced for all of his audience and were thus misunderstood, causing one of his students to commit so much negativity that he became the most powerful demon on earth. Luckily, one of his other students understood these same teachings properly and became the buddha that subjugated this demon.

In general, intentionally or unintentionally, he made many mistakes, broke his vows, and forgot his commitments to his teachers and the path. But he persevered with intense diligence, and slowly he was able to recognize his true nature. As he developed, so too did his love and concern for sentient beings—that is the way of the bodhisattva. He looked around and saw how most beings, like him, suffer from a lack of mindfulness, make mistakes, get carried away by habitual thinking, and fall away from their *samaya*—their vows and commitments. With intense empathy and understanding, he longed to achieve buddhahood to help beings rectify and repair their mistakes and downfalls.

Just before his complete enlightenment, he made his most sincere aspiration. Because he had made so many mistakes, he vowed and aspired to be the buddha that would purify all beings of whatever was obscuring them from seeing the truth. He vowed:

> When I reach buddhahood, if sentient beings, even those who have committed the five inexpiable misdeeds[3] or broken their vows, hear my name, think of me, or chant the hundred-syllable mantra, may their negativities and obscurations be purified completely. If this vow cannot be fulfilled, I will not become a buddha. May I bear witness to those who break their samaya vows so that I may purify all their negativities and obscurations.

In essence, Vajrasattva vowed to help all beings no matter how despicable the negative act or how many negative acts they have committed. Since Vajrasattva has already become a buddha, his vow must have come true, and he must have the supreme blessing power to eliminate all negative karma. When we practice Vajrasattva, we cultivate his qualities, his antidote. As long as we visualize Buddha Vajrasattva and chant the mantra in the proper way, karmic obscurations from beginningless time will surely be purified.

VAJRASATTVA'S SPECIAL POTENCY

Vajrasattva practice is the most effective of all the purification methods. This is not only because of Vajrasattva's vow but also because Vajrasattva embodies all the manifestations of enlightenment. As Patrul Rinpoche explains:

> The teacher Vajrasattva embodies the hundred deities in one. He is called "Vajrasattva, the single deity of the great secret." Of the whole inconceivable infinity of peaceful

and wrathful *yidam* deities, there is not one whom he does not embody.[4]

Vajrasattva is also known as "lord of the ocean of mandalas" because he embodies the enlightened body, speech, mind, qualities, and activities of all the buddhas and buddha families.

Furthermore, according to the *Guhyagarbha Tantra*, Vajrasattva is the primordial buddha. He is the buddha from whom all the others arise. The *Stainless Confession Tantra*,[5] however, says that Vajrasattva is the emanation body (*nirmanakaya*) of the absolute, or *dharmakaya*. This means that Vajrasattva is the physical manifestation of the primordial sphere. He is the absolute nature of reality in visible form. This concurs with the *Vajra Tent Tantra*,[6] where Vajrasattva says, "I, who am called Vajrasattva, will abide in an ordinary form in order to benefit others." Unlike other deities, such as Samantabhadra, who is normally considered the primordial buddha, Vajrasattva's compassion is such that he manifests in a way that makes him very accessible. Whether he is in the absolute or in the relative, the point is that he has the potency of all the buddhas. He is the primordial buddha, but his vows keep him as present and near to us as our own breath, especially when we are straying from our innate goodness. This is why Vajrasattva practice is the most supreme practice for purification.

TESTAMENTS TO VAJRASATTVA PRACTICE

You need not accept these statements of the power of Vajrasattva just because it is written here or because a few great masters or some respected texts have said this to be so. Just practice it for yourself to see the results. The great sage Milarepa (ca. 1052–1135) said, "How can you tell if confession has really purified you? You are purified if your thoughts have become positive."[7] Countless people for centuries have tried and tested the power of Vajrasattva only to find its true effectiveness. Vajrasattva practices, unlike most every other deity except perhaps Buddha Shakyamuni, can be found in all four schools of Tibetan Buddhism and in almost all lineages within the schools. Vajrasattva can even be found in certain forms of Chinese and Japanese Buddhism. This is a buddha and practice that has a broad appeal and recognition.

To give a specific example of its significance, the Shitro cycle of Karma Lingpa (fourteenth century) has become one of the most widespread teachings on the peaceful and wrathful deities and in particular what happens to us after death. Indeed it is the source of the famous *Tibetan Book of the Dead*. The Shitro text explains that a long time ago, there was a brahman who was one of the most learned scholars of his time. He attracted numerous students, especially from important families. One such student was a prince from a local kingdom. This prince was an exceptional student and quickly surpassed all the other students of the brahman. Unfortunately, his arrogance grew as large as his knowledge was vast. After some time this prince thought, "I know so much, there is no one equal to me except my own teacher. He alone surpasses me in this world." It did not take long for this thought to turn into jealousy and then for that jealousy to turn into hatred. Finally, the arrogant prince could not stand to have any rival, and he killed his teacher.

Just before he died, the brahman became completely indignant and furious that his own student could be so vicious and stupid. So as a final act of spite, the old brahman struck his arrogant student with a malicious curse. Owing to their violence toward one another, both the brahman and the prince were reborn in a frightful hell suffering unendurable pain. After an interminably long time, these two had exhausted enough of their negative karma to be born as animals. Even as animals, though, they endured the suffering of all six realms in their single bodies.

At this time, the buddhas took notice and felt great compassion for their endless suffering. Samantabhadra said that the only way for these two to be released from their karma without suffering for eons more was for them to practice the Shitro, in particular Vajrasattva and his hundred-syllable mantra. To assist, Vajrasattva manifested before them and recited the mantra. The power of this alone was enough for both of them to take rebirth in a situation where they could practice and learn the Shitro. Quickly, the brahman and the prince attained a high level of realization and were reborn in the pure realms. As a result, it is said that whoever hears the hundred-syllable mantra and the Shitro will be liberated and be prevented from falling into the lower realms.

Vajrasattva is not just for great sinners but also for practitioners of a very high level. For example, the great Atisha (982–1054) often stopped whatever he was doing in order to confess this or that downfall. Sometimes he would even get off his horse on a mountain pass so that he could do prostrations along with his confession. His disciples, seeing how difficult it was for their illustrious teacher, became very discouraged and asked Atisha, who was exceptionally accomplished, if it were possible to be free from negative thoughts altogether. To this he answered that though it was easy to keep the monastic and bodhisattva vows, he was constantly breaking the tantric vows. Fortunately, he said, though the tantric vows are difficult to maintain, tantra also provides the most skillful methods. In a single moment and through a single method, it is possible to purify numerous downfalls, even the many subtle ones. Thereafter Atisha taught them the meditation on Vajrasattva and the hundred-syllable mantra as the most skillful method for purification. Moreover, Atisha explained that practicing Vajrasattva is like casting a single stone to scatter a hundred birds. Though you may have created a demon or even acted like one yourself, through the practice of Vajrasattva you can remove not just the harmful effects of one negative action but of hundreds of negative actions at the same time. This is because Vajrasattva practice is not a slow or haphazard purification but a thorough and complete purification.

Another account of Vajrasattva's purifying power appears in the *Stainless Confession Tantra*. Samantabhadra was teaching a group of yogis and yoginis various methods for rectifying broken vows. First, he explained how the body, speech, and mind are the basis for all the commitments, the cause of their being broken, and the place where the results of the breakage will appear. He explained that because of this, they are also the means to mend the broken commitments. For example, if you were to break a commitment of the mind by, say, thinking that the Buddha's goal was to dupe his followers into giving him wealth, that might result in mental issues such as insanity or paranoia in this life or the next. If you confess and apply the proper mental understanding, Samantabhadra said, it will mitigate the result of the earlier view.

Vajrasattva was listening to this teaching and saw that this method works well when the broken vow is clearly seen and understood. Often, however, these downfalls took place in a previous life or without sufficient mindfulness to recollect them. Hence, he appeared before the assembly listening to Samantabhadra and declared that while such a teaching helps to free beings from their negativity and samsara, it is not sufficient for everyone. Then Vajrasattva said, "Take heed all you practitioners with great defilement: so that you may purify, I will recite this hundred-syllable mantra!" Thereafter he explained that all the buddhas of the past went through this path of confession and that it will lead all future practitioners to buddhahood.

What We Accomplish through Vajrasattva Practice

THE PRACTICE OF VAJRASATTVA accomplishes two goals. First, it helps us to overcome our bad habits, wrong actions, and deluded views. By overcoming these obscurations and imprints, it is possible to experience all positive circumstances and conditions. In other words, when we combine proper motivation, correct understanding, and vibrantly real visualizations, the relative benefits are as stupendous as the great texts all say. One Indian text describes the benefits this way:

Whoever chants the hundred syllables
is not struck by sickness, pain, or early death.

Whoever chants the hundred syllables
is not beset by poverty or woe.
His enemies are crushed
and all his wishes are fulfilled.

Whoever chants the hundred syllables
obtains a son if a son he wants
or wealth if wealth he wants.
If land he lacks, then land he gains.

Whoever wants longevity
should chant the hundred syllables,
and, when he thinks his years are spent,
he'll find three hundred more are sent!
The same man, happy in this world,
in Sukhavati will be born.

Whoever chants the hundred syllables,
is safe from [harmful] dakinis, spirits, and zombies
and from the demons of defilement and forgetfulness.

If he recites the hundred syllables,
an evildoer, too, will see the Buddha.

If he recites the hundred syllables,
a fool will gain intelligence,
a luckless man turn fortunate,
change and frustration will be destroyed,
the worst wrongdoer, purified.

In this and other lives as well,
he will a universal monarch be
and, finally, in freedom rest
and buddhahood attain.[8]

The second goal we can accomplish, as mentioned above, is full buddhahood. This is the real reason to practice. All the relative benefits disappear at death, but liberation will free us from all suffering, even death itself. It says in the tantra *Compendium of Truths*, "It is a great protection for us to recite the mantra of Guru Vajrasattva even a single time, whereupon we will obtain the supreme siddhi [enlightenment] in one instant." Even if we do not have that strength, and it takes many repetitions, this practice makes possible the realization of the true nature of the mind and the true nature of reality. This is because through Vajrasattva practice we remove impure perceptions, through which our pure awareness is revealed, and this pure awareness then further clears away impurities, which makes possible a deeper understanding of pure awareness, until ultimately there are no more impurities. Then naturally we are pure awareness, which is to say completely enlightened.

THE POTENCY OF THE HUNDRED-SYLLABLE MANTRA

Specifically, as the previous quote on the relative and absolute benefits states, it is through the hundred-syllable mantra that the diligent Vajrasattva practitioner can realize all the common and extraordinary accomplishments. The hundred-syllable mantra is the essence of Vajrasattva and the Vajrasattva practice.

As the name suggests, there are a hundred syllables in this mantra, one for each of the hundred deities of the Shitro. Each syllable is a representation of each of the heart syllables of all the hundred peaceful and wrathful deities. Since Vajrasattva's heart mantra contains all the other deities' heart syllables, Vajrasattva pervades all the enlightened spheres; Vajrasattva is the heart essence of all the mandalas, the "lord of the ocean of mandalas." As such, Patrul Rinpoche proclaimed, "The hundred-syllable mantra is superior to all other mantras; you must know that there is no more profound practice than this."[9]

The benefits and power of the hundred-syllable mantra are simply innumerable. The *Stainless Confession Tantra* says:

> The hundred-syllable mantra is the essence of all the buddhas' wisdom, and it can purify all the obscurations of broken precepts and conceptual thoughts. It is the king of purification. If one continuously recites it 108 times at one meditation session, all the broken precepts will be

restored, and one will obtain liberation from the three lower realms. Any practitioner who aspires to recite this mantra will not only be watched and protected as the most favorite child by the buddhas of the three times in this lifetime but also become the favorite child of all the buddhas in future lifetimes.

Moreover, according to the *Essential Ornament*:

> To recite correctly twenty-one times
> the hundred-syllable mantra
> while clearly visualizing Vajrasattva
> seated on a white lotus and moon
> constitutes the blessing of the downfalls,
> which are thus kept from increasing.
> Thus the great siddhas have taught.
> So practice it always.
> If you recite it a hundred thousand times,
> you will become the very embodiment of utter purity.[10]

The Guhyasamaja commentaries concur, saying that by reciting the hundred-syllable mantra just twenty-one times, negative karma will not multiply and the mind will be blessed. These commentaries also agree that by reciting the hundred-syllable mantra one hundred thousand times, it will completely purify all negative karma, even the negative karma accrued by a fully ordained person breaking every vow.

It is not only the hundred-syllable mantra that will bring these great benefits. Even the short six-syllable mantra of Vajrasattva, *Om vajra sattva hum*, has immense benefit. It is said in a liturgy of Vajrasattva practice, "The six-syllable mantra of Guru Vajrasattva is the nature of all the buddhas of the three times. Only those who have offered and served countless buddhas can get the opportunity to hear it, through which they will take rebirth in the land of Vajra-sattva, obtain the blessings of all buddhas, enter the Mahayana path, and obtain clairvoyance and the supreme wisdom eye." Furthermore, the *Vajradhara Tantra* says, "If one properly recites this mantra one hundred thousand times, serious wrongs such as breaking the root vows can be purified utterly."

CONCLUSION

Our habituation to emotional and self-centered ways of being, to negativity and distortion, hinders our vision and understanding of our true nature more than anything else. Without washing away the murkiness that covers our diamond-like pure awareness, it is nearly impossible to find our innate discipline, concentration, or wisdom, let alone the extraordinary accomplishments, rebirth in Sukhavati pure land, or complete enlightenment. The compassionate Buddha was unable to bear the perpetual confusion that leads to misdeeds and its resultant suffering and so taught all kinds of purification methods and practices. Among all of them, the most effective is to visualize Vajrasattva and to chant his mantras. This is because Vajrasattva is the primordial buddha in physical form and the embodiment of all the enlightened buddhas, deities, and mandalas. To practice Vajrasattva is to follow in the footsteps of all the buddhas, since all buddhas have attained buddhahood through this practice. With this understanding, we can begin the actual practice with trust and determination.

The Main Practice

PREPARING FOR PRACTICE

IT IS ESSENTIAL we begin with a suitable motivation. We undertake this purification to release not only ourselves from the grip of suffering but all beings. Without this motivation, it would be like running from a burning house without waking our family and loved ones. We cannot really be free if our loved ones are still suffering. And, because we have migrated through countless lives, every being must have been a dearly loved relation at one time or another. Therefore it is not satisfying to simply purify ourselves alone for our own sake. To truly purify and liberate ourselves, we must think of all our loved ones. With this motivation in place, the merit of our practice multiplies infinitely. Then we can apply the correct understanding of the power of Vajrasattva and the significance of purification we have just discussed. Finally, we visualize and recite to the best of our ability, constantly trying to bring the visualized images out of haziness and into magnificence.

HOW TO RECITE THE MANTRA

The primary support for the practice of Vajrasattva, as the *Essential Ornament* stated above, is proper recitation of the mantra. The benefit that you can get from this mantra does not depend so much on the quantity as on the quality of the recitation. As indicated above in the *Compendium of Truths* quote, it takes only one recitation to achieve the ultimate accomplishment. So when it says that by reciting the mantra a hundred thousand times, or even just once, you will become totally pure, it does not mean recitations done with distraction or half-heartedly, which are relatively easy to accumulate. If that were the case, anyone who completed the common preliminary practices would already be enlightened. For that matter, there would be no need for the preliminary practices: anyone, given three months, could become "the finest of all the buddhas' heirs." Not to mention, there would be no need to publish, let alone read, this book!

How much negative karma we are able to wash away depends very much on *how* we recite this mantra. Just because the hundred-syllable mantra is the most potent mantra for purification, and thereby liberation, it does not mean that the mantra alone does all of the work. We do not continue to let our minds run wild through all manner of fantasies while our mouths mumble some pleasant sounds. The point is to tame our wild minds with the help and support and compassion of Vajrasattva and the hundred-syllable mantra.

When reciting the mantra, it should not be too soft or too loud. It is often recommended to recite it at "collar length." This means that if someone were to put their ear at the edge of your collar or lapel, only then would they be able to hear you. Saying the mantra silently will not allow the mantra to vibrate through your subtle or gross body and thus will slow down the process of purification. Saying the mantra too loudly will "agitate phenomena," which can upset everyone from the person sitting next to you to spirits or ethereal beings. These phenomena may then deem it necessary to disturb your practice and hinder your purification! Thus it is best to recite in such a way that while you can still feel your voice reverberating through your body, it is not so loud as to disturb anyone seen or unseen.

To keep count of the mantra recitations, it is good to have a mala. A *mala* is a necklace of beads, like a rosary. Many are made from seeds of a bodhi tree, the type of tree under which the Buddha was enlightened. For Vajrasattva practice, a crystal mala is also good, since it signifies purity. If these are difficult to find, you may use a mala of wood. For Vajrasattva practice, it is best to avoid using bone or *rudraksha* malas, as these are intended for more wrathful practices.

A mala generally has 108 beads — one for each of the hundred peaceful and wrathful deities of the Shitro and eight extra to make up for any mistakes — plus one large bead called the *guru bead*. This guru bead represents the teacher, who is more important than any of the other deities or buddhas because it is the guru who introduces you to all the buddhas. The string that runs through all the beads represents the unity and the link between all the deities, the guru, and you. Thus the mala is not just a necklace but your most central practice support and so is best treated with great respect. In other words, avoid stepping on it, walking over it, or leaving it on the floor in general, and also avoid twirling it or using it as an abacus. When using the mala, place it in your left hand, resting it on the top of your index finger and keep your hand close to your heart area. To keep count, begin with the guru bead, and then pull each bead down and toward your body, counting one bead for each mantra that you finish. When you return again to the guru bead, this counts as one hundred recitations.

HOW TO START

With our minds full of faith, compassion, and understanding, we are ready to begin the main practice of Vajrasattva. Each picture and facing page is one step of the visualization process. It may at first seem strange and difficult to keep all these images and especially the Tibetan letters in mind while still reciting the prayers and mantras. In time, and with some effort, though, it will become easy and natural.

A good way to begin is to simply familiarize yourself with the pictures in this book. You may want to take the picture of Vajrasattva alone and look at it until it has imprinted itself on your consciousness. If you can get to where you can still see the image when you close your eyes, you will find it easier to generate the visualization during the practice.

Often the most difficult parts of the visualization will be the letters of the hundred-syllable mantra encircling the heart syllable. Do not worry if this is too much. Focus mainly on the heart syllable and simply feel that the full mantra is there surrounding it. The more you practice and the more you purify, the easier it will be to visualize all the details. The idea is to apply this practice to the best of your ability. So long as you trust in Vajrasattva, reflect on the need for purification and the four opponent powers, and maintain the wish to benefit others, your practice will progress and you will be removing immense amounts of negative karma for yourself and all sentient beings.

Do not worry if you cannot maintain a clear and perfect visualization, understanding, or motivation for this practice. What makes Vajrasattva so potent is that just by reciting his name, we are confessing our inability to see him clearly or practice him properly. This does not mean that we do not try again and again to generate faith and a motivation to benefit others. This also does not mean that we can be lazy and distracted through 107 recitations and then think that by putting some effort into the final recitation we are really doing quality practice. The more we recall Vajrasattva's name and form, the more we purify our inability to do just that. This is Vajrasattva's vow and his exceptional quality.

There is a great potential for transformation and benefit in this practice and these pages, but it is still up to you to apply it fully. The pictures are given as a support, a rough starting place, but the real depth of the practice comes when your visualization is clear enough that you no longer need the pictures. At that point, the practice will come alive, and you will start to see Vajrasattva everywhere and in everyone. Since this is everyone's ultimate nature, it will be as though you are seeing the true nature of reality in its purity.

PHYSICAL PREPARATION

Now that you have understood the power of Vajrasattva and the necessity and means for purification, it is time to practice. First, it is important to find a quiet location where there are few disturbances. This way it will be easier to concentrate and reflect. It is best, if possible, to sit on the floor. To be more comfortable a mat is ideal, and if that is too strenuous, a cushion may also be used. Having the rear of your cushion raised up a bit makes it easier to sit up straight for long periods. The position of the body is instrumental in our ability to calm the body and mind. According to Kamalashila's *Stages of Meditation*, there are eight important facets of the posture most conducive to meditation:

1. Place the legs in cross-legged vajra position. This is sometimes called the lotus posture. Basically it is like the sitting position of the Buddha. The half-lotus position, where only one foot is on the opposite thigh, is also acceptable. The simple cross-legged position, where neither foot is on a thigh, is allowed if the others are too painful or difficult. Further allowances are made for those with injuries to sit on a chair, but if you do so, try to keep both feet flat on the floor.

2. Keep the eyes relaxed, not open too widely or closed tightly. Set their focus toward the tip of the nose, though not so much that you are cross-eyed.

3. Do not lean the body backward or forward, but sit straight and even with the vertebrae resting balanced one upon the other in

an erect column, drawing your attention inward. Sitting straight dispels dullness, excitement, sleepiness, and forgetting the meditation. It also helps to maintain the meditation session longer.

4. Keep the shoulders even, straight, and relaxed.
5. Do not tilt the head upward or downward or skew it to one side. Straighten the body from the level of the navel to the level of the nose.
6. Let the teeth and lips rest in their natural position.
7. Touch the tongue to the roof of the mouth.
8. Breathe gently.

MENTAL PREPARATION

Once we are seated comfortably and in accordance with the eight aspects, it is useful to reflect on our situation and condition. By thinking about our good fortune in finding the causes and conditions to practice, we cultivate joy for the practice. Recognizing that we do not have much time in this life and we still have many karmic seeds to purify that will otherwise lead us back into suffering and far less fortunate situations, we develop the courage and enthusiasm to practice as diligently as we can. This joy and diligence will help us to keep our commitment and discipline in the practice when it is difficult and frustrating. In order to accomplish this, we reflect on what are called the four thoughts that change the mind or the four thoughts of renouncing *samsara*, cyclic existence. We reflect on these four thoughts before taking refuge. For new practitioners who have never contemplated these thoughts before, your teacher will instruct you to reflect on them repeatedly with detailed explanations until real experience arises. If you have no teacher present, there are thorough explanations in books such as *Words of My Perfect Teacher* that would be good to read and contemplate again and again.

For those already familiar with these four contemplations, here is an abbreviated explanation as a reminder.

The freedoms and advantages of a human body

It is extremely difficult to obtain a wish-fulfilling human body with the freedoms and advantages even once, let alone again and again. It is the most meaningful support; so when we possess it, we should use it wisely and practice the holy Dharma for the ultimate benefit and happiness of all sentient beings.

The impermanence of life

Once we have this precious life, it is like lightning in the sky. Death is certain, but the time of death is uncertain. Therefore we should devote ourselves to Dharma practice without delay.

At death, our food, wealth, property, loved ones, enemies, houses, and body cannot follow us, nor can they benefit or harm us. No matter whether we have had success or failure, happiness or suffering, in this life, everything we have amassed becomes superfluous and meaningless at that moment of death.

The karmic law of cause and effect

Nonetheless, positive and negative karma follows us always like a shadow. It will never leave us even after we die. We cannot discard any of the negative karma we have committed. We cannot experience any positive results we have not created the causes for. No matter where we take rebirth, whether in the higher or lower realms, we will still be in cyclic existence, where there is no true happiness or peace at all. If we are honest with ourselves, we cannot be certain that we will avoid falling into the lower realms in the future. Therefore, from now on, even if our life is endangered, we will endeavor to avoid creating any negative karma and diligently accumulate positive karma alone.

The disadvantages of cyclic existence

If we take rebirth in a higher realm thanks to our contaminated positive karma, it will appear that we have some happiness and peace. However, this is like a dream, which disappears very soon. Everything in cyclic existence is subject to change; nothing is permanent. No matter how wonderful cyclic existence is, it has no essence. Only Dharma practice can help us escape meaninglessly experiencing the endless suffering of samsara.

Reflect on these repeatedly from the depth of your heart and practice accordingly. The more effort put into these reflections and into the actual practice, the more certain and profound the results.

Visualizing Vajrasattva
THE POWER OF RELIANCE

IN THE SPACE in front of you, visualize the syllable *ah* and then chant it slowly. The syllable *ah* symbolizes the ultimate nature of the *dharmadhatu*, the realm of all phenomena. In this way, it represents both freedom from attachment and the unborn emptiness. Since all phenomena have no real entities, they do not truly exist, and thus their nature is emptiness. Since they do not truly exist, there is no arising. Without arising, there is nothing born, and thus they are unborn.

When chanting the syllable *ah*, abide in the great pure emptiness of equality. The equality here means that there is no self-nature and so there is no differentiation. It is pure because there is no attachment and no mental affliction. To rest in such a state, one abides without any conceptual thoughts. This is called the *shamatha of suchness*. For those who have some recognition of the nature of mind, they should abide in the corresponding states.

Then visualize on that lotus a perfectly round moon disc, which looks like the full moon on the fifteenth day of the lunar month. This moon disc represents the absence of all faults and the presence of all good qualities — the perfection of purification and realization.

Instantaneously, like a shooting star, a brilliant white *hum* syllable appears on the moon disc. This *hum* indicates the inseparability of emptiness and enlightenment.

The blessings of the body, speech, mind, good qualities, and activities of all the buddhas in the ten directions, as well as all the wisdom, compassion, strength, and essence of the entire sentient world, completely sink into and infuse the syllable *hum*, which appears brilliantly radiant, like having completely woken up from a dream. This is called *meditating with a single-pointed mind on the subtle seed syllable.*

Instantaneously, the *hum* transforms into your incomparable and glorious root guru, whose nature is the treasure of compassion. He takes the enjoyment body, or *sambhogakaya*, form of Vajrasattva, whose entity is one with the hundred peaceful and wrathful deities.

This Vajrasattva is white in color, like a snowy mountain peak lit by a hundred thousand suns. His body is clear like the reflection of the moon in water, or like an image reflected in a mirror—he appears yet has no intrinsic existence. He has one face and two arms. His right hand holds in front of his heart the five-pronged vajra of awareness and emptiness. His left hand, near his left hip, grasps the bell of appearance and emptiness. His two legs are crossed in the vajra position, and he is adorned with the thirteen adornments of a sambhogakaya—five silken garments and eight ornaments (see below). His body emanates immeasurable white wisdom rays that spread to all the worlds in the ten directions. This is called *meditating with a single-pointed mind on the gross deity body.*

▪ The knot of hair on the top of his head symbolizes that he has never been confused or distracted and his continuum has always been full of great wisdom.

▪ His singular face represents the sole heartdrop of ultimate dharmakaya. "Sole" means everything is included in it. Heartdrops can fall into two categories: ultimate and conventional. The ultimate refers to dharmakaya.

▪ His two eyes represent the wisdom of suchness and omniscience. The wisdom of suchness is to realize the nature of all phenomena as emptiness. The wisdom of omniscience is to understand all phenomena.

▪ His two ears are the union of the two truths: conventional truth and ultimate truth.

▪ His two nostrils represent benefitting self and others effortlessly.

▪ His lips symbolize universal great happiness.

▪ His teeth represent the perfect mandala of the forty-two peaceful deities.

▪ His tongue signifies the union of samsara and nirvana.

▪ His two arms show the equality of wisdom and compassion.

▪ His ten fingers represent the five buddha bodies and five wisdoms.[11]

▪ His two feet symbolize not abiding in either samsara or nirvana.

▪ The twelve joints of his body represent the purification of the transmigration through the twelve links of dependent origination.

▪ His ten toes represent the five perfect male buddhas and five perfect female buddhas of the five directions.[12]

▪ Sitting in the vajra posture signifies being free from the drifting and changing nature of the three times.

▪ His complete body represents the enlightened body with all the good qualities.

▪ The wisdom rays radiating from his pores denote the 84,000 teachings.

THE THIRTEEN SAMBHOGAKAYA ADORNMENTS

The five silken garments are:
1. Headband
2. Upper garment
3. Long scarf
4. Belt
5. Lower garment

The eight ornaments are:
6. Crown
7. Earrings
8. Short necklace
9. Armlets
10. Two longer necklaces of different lengths
11. Bracelets on each wrist
12. Anklets on each foot
13. Rings on each foot

The thirteen sambhogakaya adornments signify empathy for sentient beings through great compassion. They also represent the ability to manifest what is pure and beautiful without the need for pacifying the five desires.

The five silken garments correspond to the conquest of the five afflictive emotions.

The eight jewel ornaments denote the eightfold noble path: right view, right thought, right speech, right conduct, right livelihood, right effort, right mindfulness, and right meditative concentration.

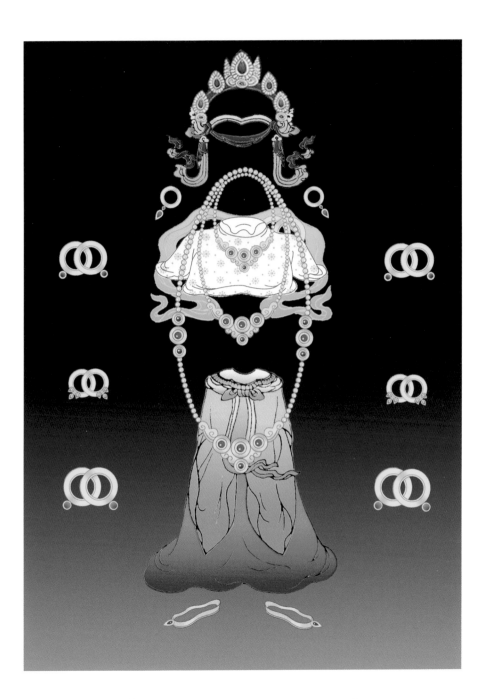

According to the *Esoteric Inner Tantra*, the vajra in his right hand represents the ultimate eternal vajra, the supremely skillful means. The upper five prongs are the five male buddhas of the five directions, and the lower five prongs are the five female buddhas of the five directions. The upper and lower lotus leaves symbolize the bodhisattvas, male and female, the bead garland corresponds to the peaceful deities, and the center grip is the unsurpassed dharmadhatu palace, which is free from all conceptual fabrication.

Also based on the *Esoteric Inner Tantra*, the bell in his left hand represents the supreme wisdom, so the upper part of the bell has the face of the female buddha Freedom of the Vajradhatu. The half vajra on the top of the bell signifies the union of bliss and emptiness.

The eight lotuses on the bell have eight seed syllables respectively, which indicate all the female buddhas and female bodhisattvas except the female buddha Freedom of the Vajradhatu. The half necklace and the two circles of vertically and horizontally arranged vajras represent using the supremely skillful means to ornament the supreme wisdom.

Some bells have the syllables *om, ah, hum* on the inner surface to represent the body, speech, and mind of the buddha. The bell clapper is said to be the source of great bliss or the obtainable wisdom. The round space inside the bell stands for the emptiness of the dharmadhatu, which is free from all conceptual fabrication.

This completes the first section of the practice. By taking refuge, generating bodhichitta, and visualizing the deity, we establish the first of the four opponent powers—the power of reliance.

If we have approached this with a genuine mind of reliance on the noble deity and with bodhichitta, the true intention to benefit countless sentient beings, and we have clearly visualized the noble deity, we can cultivate a very strong power of reliance for purification. Thus our foundation for purification can be very strong.

Now chant the verse for visualizing the noble deity once:

Ah

In front of me, in an ocean of vast offering clouds,
appears Lord Vajrasattava,
white like the moon,
upon a lotus and moon seat.
With one face and his two hands holding the bell
    and vajra,
he sits in full lotus with the perfect
    sambhogakaya adornments
and emanates rays of wisdom throughout
    the ten directions.

Visualize these clearly with a pure and calm mind.

Supplicating Vajrasattva
THE POWER OF REGRET

After visualizing the noble deity clearly, pray diligently to Guru Vajrasattva. The dharmakaya of Vajrasattva pervades all worlds throughout the ten directions. His aspirations spread universally in all times and spaces. As genuine and firm as a diamond, he never deceives us. He is an everlasting, reliable field of refuge, but his blessing can only infuse the mindstream of those who pray to him wholeheartedly. Therefore we now pray devoutly to open our mindstream so that we are able to receive his blessings through the power of his aspiration. The more honestly, intensely, and thoroughly we pray, the deeper, sooner, and stronger the blessing we receive from him. Thus pray:

> Alas, Guru Vajrasattva, please recall the aspirations you made, we, your helpless children in the ocean of three realms, who have experienced for eons and eons endless and incomparable suffering, such as the three kinds of sufferings and eight kinds of sufferings,[13] beseech you to bless us with your great loving-kindness and compassion. Please take care of us and never abandon us!

Then confess in this way:

From beginningless time until now,
influenced by attachment, hatred, and ignorance,
I have with acts of body, speech, and mind
knowingly and unknowingly committed so many misdeeds,
both natural and those designated so by the Buddha,
such as the ten nonvirtues, the five inexpiable misdeeds,
and the five similarly inexpiable wrongdoings,
thus violating the precepts of the three vehicles and so on.

Reflect on these misdeeds one by one. Confess without hiding or concealing any of them, and generate a deep sense of repentance as though you have just ingested poison and are in the subsequent mental state of regret and dread.

Afterward, request Guru Vajrasattva's blessings:

Please take care of me with your great wisdom.
Please watch over me with your compassionate eyes.
Please listen to my confession with your divine ears.
Today I have nothing good to tell,
only all the countless wrong actions I have committed from
    beginningless time.

Now I will confess in the correct way:
Please cleanse and purify all my negative karma right now.
Please grant your blessings to destroy all my negative karma
before I finish this meditation session.

Guru Vajrasattva is very compassionate. He will not think less of us due to our heavy load of negative karma. The more willing, sincere, thorough, and straightforward our confession, the more directly, swiftly, and strongly his blessings will descend on us.

In this way, we establish the second of the four opponent powers—the power of regret.

Promising Vajrasattva

THE POWER OF RESOLVE

Next, in front of Vajrasattva, aspire with deep conviction to refrain from any negative actions by thinking or saying aloud:

From now on, even if my life is in danger I will never commit any negative action.

Without this power of resolve, the continuum of the negative karma cannot be thoroughly severed.

It is far from adequate to merely say that we will refrain from committing negative karma. We must thoroughly examine the ten nonvirtues one by one and vow to not commit each one of them. Moreover, we should never encourage others to commit them nor rejoice when they do commit them. For example, when we take the vow of abstaining from killing, we vow not to kill any creature, from those that are big like lions, tigers, and human beings, to those that are small, such as lice, mosquitoes, flies, and the like.

In this way we generate the third power of the four opponent powers—the power of resolve.

RECITING THE MANTRA
THE POWER OF THE REMEDY

IN THE NEXT STEP, we recite the hundred-syllable mantra and the short mantra of Vajrasattva to counteract negative karma. In general, in order to counteract any negative karma that we have accumulated in the past, we can perform virtuous actions, such as prostrating to the buddhas and bodhisattvas, rejoicing in others' merits and virtues, dedicating virtue to obtain enlightenment, and guarding and maintaining the primordial nature of the mind. These are all antidotes for purifying the intrinsic misdeeds and the misdeeds designated by the Buddha. Here, though, we focus on mindfully reciting the king of mantras—the hundred-syllable mantra—and the short mantra of Vajrasattva. By this we complete the fourth of the opponent powers—the power of the remedy.

We often easily commit negative actions out of indolence or lack of mindful awareness. At these times, we should not simply ignore them but purify them using the four opponent powers, as we have just gone through.

When we practice purification, how many of the negative actions can be purified or whether they will be thoroughly removed or only slightly uprooted depends entirely on the quality of our confession. It depends on whether we have a very strong mind of purification, whether the four opponent powers are complete, and whether the time we spend on purification is continuous and long enough. The more fervently we perform these acts, the greater the effects of our purification.

Among the four opponent powers, the power of regret and the power of resolve are motivated by reflecting on the law of cause and effect. By reflecting repeatedly on the disadvantages that negative actions bring later, we develop strong regret and a determination to avoid further nonvirtuous deeds. In this way, our purification reaches fruition.

Next we pray, remembering the four opponent powers:

Oh, Guru Vajrasattva,
please recall your great aspiration in the past.
I and other suffering sentient beings supplicate you.
Please keep us in your care with great compassion.
From beginningless time until now,
we have committed many evils with body, speech,
    and mind.
As though I had taken poison,
I now deeply regret them and thoroughly confess
    them all.
From now on, even if it costs me my life,
I will never commit any nonvirtuous acts.

We now begin the practice of reciting the hundred-syllable mantra.

In the heart of Guru Vajrasattva, who is an arrow's length above your head exactly as described before, visualize a small white lotus disc. Upon this lotus is a white moon disc the size of a flattened mustard seed. Upon that is a white vajra standing straight up. At the grip of the vajra is a white *hum* finely drawn as though with a strand of hair.

Visualize every syllable in the hundred-syllable mantra standing straight up without touching each other, encircling the *hum* at the center. Recite the hundred-syllable mantra once as a prayer. You may recite according to the Tibetan pronunciation of the Sanskrit syllables:

Om benza sato samaya / manu palaya /
benza sato tenopa / tita dido may bhawa /
suto kayo may bhawa / supo kayo may bhawa /
anu rakto may bhawa / sarwa siddhi mempra yatsa /
sarwa karma sutsa may / tsitam shriyam kuru hum /
ha ha ha ha ho bhagawan / sarwa tathagata /
benza ma may muntsa / benza bhawa / maha samaya sato ah

Or according to Sanskrit phonetics:

Om Vajrasattva, samayam anupalaya!
Vajrasattva tvenopatishta! Dridho me bhava!
Sutoshyo me bhava! Suposhyo me bhava!
Anurakto me bhava! Sarva siddhim me prayaccha!
Sarva karmasu cha me! Chittam shreya kuru, hum!
Ha ha ha ha ho! Bhagavan, sarva tathagata,
vajra ma me muncha! Vajribhava mahasamayasattva ah!

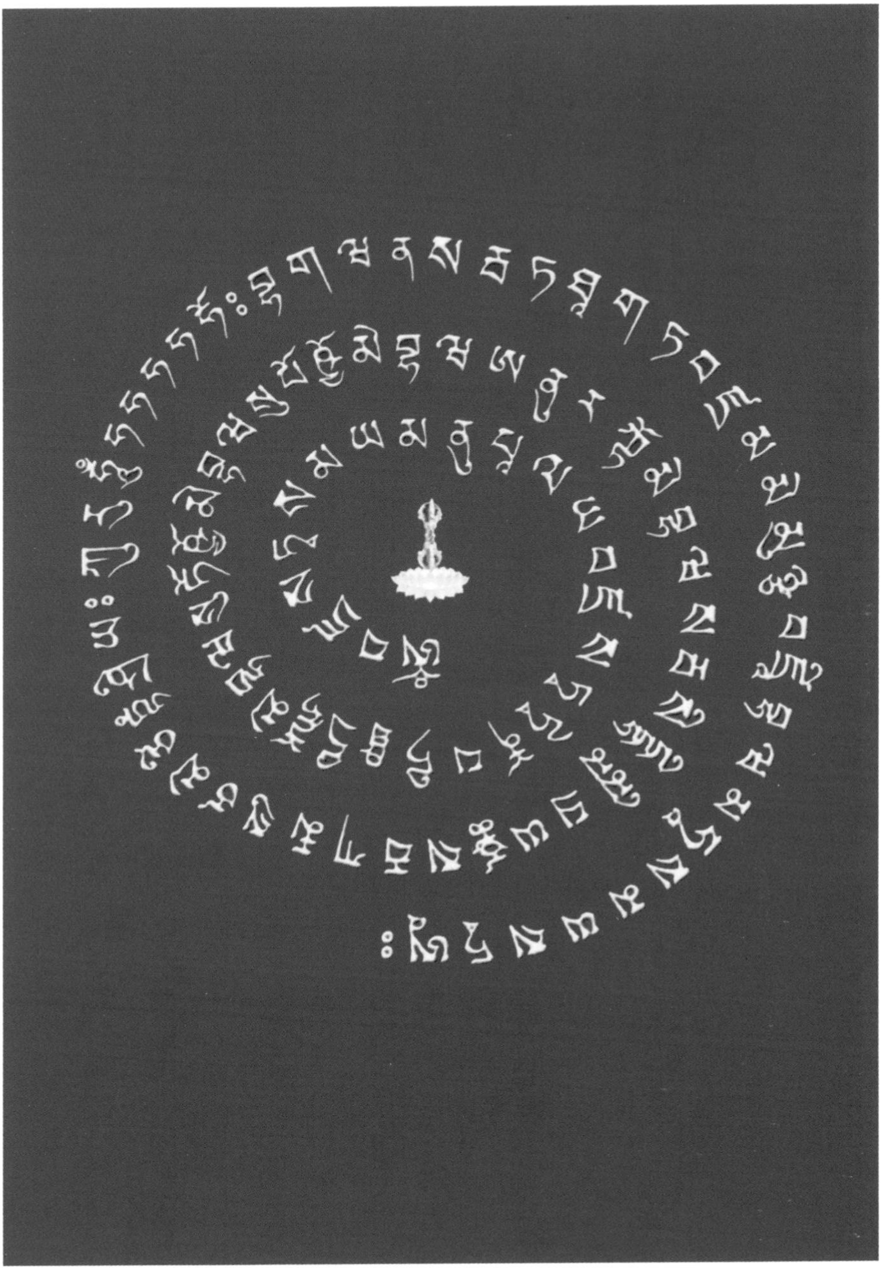

Then, while reciting the mantra softly and continuously, visualize white nectar of wisdom and compassion descending continuously from all the body parts of Guru Vajrasattva and the mantra disc in his heart as well as the lotus and moon disc he sits upon. This nectar enters through the crown of the head into you and all other sentient beings.

Imagine that the enormous burden of negative actions, committed through the body, speech, and mind of yourself and other sentient beings from beginningless time turns into black liquid, liquid coal, dust, smoke, clouds and vapors, and so forth and is expelled from the body.

Envisage the earth beneath you opening up, and at the same time, like an unstoppable flood, the stream of white nectar cleans away all the blood, pus, frogs, black liquid, and so forth. Visualize them freely gushing from the soles of your feet, from your anus, and from all your pores and flowing down into the earth.

In the crack in the earth, visualize Yama, the lord of death, with his hair standing straight up. He is surrounded by all the beings, male and female, to whom you owe karmic debts as well as all those seeking revenge on you. Their mouths are open wide and their arms reach out with grasping hands.

Visualize that the pus, blood, frogs, smoke, black liquid, and so forth all run into their mouths, arms, and hands. At the same time, recite the hundred-syllable mantra with great compassion, remembering that all the buddhas and bodhisattvas are continuously bestowing the nectar of wisdom and compassion to purify you.

If time allows, meditate on this visualization and recitation repeatedly. This is very important for practitioners who are genuinely concerned about the quality of their practice. How long this continues depends on the level of the practitioner.

After this, Yama and all the debtors and foes below you underground are appeased and satisfied, and so their resentment is melted away, the debts are cleared, and the negative obscurations are purified. Therefore the lord of death and all the rest close their mouths and hands and lower their arms. The rift in the earth closes up.

You can visualize all the above steps simultaneously or you can visualize alternately. For example, when you recite the hundred-syllable mantra, you can sometimes concentrate on visualizing just the face of Vajrasattva and sometimes his arms and hands.

Likewise, sometimes you can concentrate on the vajra and bell in his hands, sometimes you can concentrate on his necklaces, and sometimes his anklets and the rings on his feet.

You can concentrate on the thirteen sambhogakaya adornments of Guru Vajrasattva. At other times, visualize the nectar descending from Guru Vajrasattva, purifying all negative obstacles and negative obscurations. Then sometimes focus on the power of regret for digging out the seeds of negative karma and the power of resolve for cutting the continuum of negative karma.

At the end of this recitation, visualize your body and the bodies of all other beings as having become transparent like clear crystal but with a luminous quality.

Receiving Blessings and Empowerments

For the next part, visualize a long tube, like a fluorescent light, going from the top of your head to about four fingers below the navel. This tube is straight, luminous, sheer, and about the width of your thumb. This is your central channel.

At each of the four centers of your body, visualize that this channel branches out into four umbrella-like wheels, or *chakras*. At the level of your navel is the wheel of manifestation, with sixty-four channel petals or spokes curving upward. At the level of your heart is the wheel of Dharma, with eight channel petals curving downward. At the level of your throat is the wheel of enjoyment, with sixteen channel petals curving upward. At the crown of your head is the wheel of great bliss, with thirty-two channel petals curving downward.

Again the nectar of wisdom and compassion descends from Vajrasattva. Imagine that the white nectar completely fills the wheel of great bliss at the crown of your head, the wheel of enjoyment at your throat, the wheel of Dharma at your heart, and the wheel of manifestation at your navel.

Then the nectar spreads out through the four wheels into every part of the body, beginning to fill it like a glass.

The whole body, including fingers and toes, is full of white nectar, and looks like a crystal vase full of milk.

When the nectar descends to the wheel of great bliss at your crown, you and all sentient beings obtain the vase empowerment. Having purified all karmic obscurations, the wisdom of joy arises in your mental continuum, and the fruit of nirmanakaya is obtained.

Next, when the nectar descends to the wheel of enjoyment at your throat, you and all sentient beings obtain the secret empowerment. With all the obscurations of afflictive emotions purified, the wisdom of supreme joy arises in your mental continuum, and the fruit of sambhogakaya is obtained.

Then, when the nectar descends to the wheel of Dharma at your heart, you and all sentient beings obtain the wisdom empowerment. Now all the cognitive obscurations are purified, and so the wisdom of extreme joy arises in your mental continuum, and the fruit of dharmakaya is obtained.

Finally, when the nectar descends to the wheel of manifestation at your navel, you and all sentient beings obtain the word empowerment. Having purified all the karmic obscurations, the wisdom of innate joy arises in your mental continuum, and the fruit of *svabhavikaya*, the pure essence body, is obtained.

In summary, remember that Guru Vajrasattva looks at you with eyes of compassion. He gives empowerments with a gentle hand full of blessings and grants the liberation from all kinds of negative karma, especially the negative obscurations caused by breaking *samaya* vows and commitments. Through this, you and all sentient beings accomplish the *siddhi*, or attainment, of both worldly perfection and transcendental merit at each of the different stages and paths.

Then recite the verse for confessing and the verse for requesting the bestowal of siddhi.

The verse for confessing

O protector!
Out of stupidity and ignorance, I have not kept
    my samaya properly.
Guru protector! Vajradhara! I pray to you for
    protection and liberation.
Guru of all sentient beings, your nature is great
    compassion.
To you, I go for refuge.

The verse for accomplishing siddhi

Please watch us with your compassionate eyes,
bestow liberation with your gentle hand,
and purify the samaya that I and other sentient
    beings break or lose.
Grant us all the common and uncommon
    supreme siddhis now.

I and other sentient beings have broken and lost the major
and minor samaya pledges of body, speech, and mind. For
all these we confess deeply. I beg you, please cleanse and
purify all our karmic obscurations, negative obscurations,
and other stains.

Guru Vajrasattva is delighted and says with a smile, "Noble sons and noble daughters, all the negative obscurations you have accumulated are purified completely." Thus he bestows purification.

Guru Vajrasattva then dissolves into light, which then dissolves into your body.

As this light from Guru Vajrasattva dissolves into your body, you and all sentient beings transform into Buddha Vajrasattva, who is transparent, white as the moon, with one face, two hands holding a bell and vajra, wearing the sambhogakaya adornments, sitting in the vajra position, and radiating wisdom light in all directions.

The Short Mantra

Then, in Vajrasattva's heart sits a moon disc as small as a flattened mustard seed. In the center sits a blue syllable *hum*, in front of which is a white syllable *om*. On the right is a yellow syllable *vajra*, in the back is a red syllable *sa*, and on the left is a green syllable *tva*. Now recite the short mantra: *Om vajra sattva hum.*

The five syllables radiate light upward in their respective colors of white, yellow, red, green, and blue.

At the ends of the rays of light are the goddess of happiness and other offering goddesses. Their hands radiate countless offerings, such as the eight auspicious symbols, the seven jewels of the universal monarch, fringed parasols, victory banners, canopies, thousand-spoke golden wheels, and right-spiraling conch shells.

All these countless offerings are offered to the innumerable buddhas and bodhisattvas of the inconceivable and boundless worlds, which pleases them immensely. By this offering, you perfect the accumulations and purify negative obstacles.

Then visualize that the great compassion and blessings of all the buddhas and bodhisattvas turns into light rays of different colors, which then dissolve into your body and the bodies of all sentient beings.

All the material worlds transform into the Land of Manifest Joy (Abhirata), the pure land of Vajrasattva. All sentient beings become Vajrasattvas in one of the five colors of white, yellow, red, green, or blue.

This Land of Manifest Joy is filled with the hum of all the Vajrasattvas reciting *Om vajra sattva hum*. This visualization creates the condition for the realization of your rupakaya, your enlightened form, by which you can benefit others.

Recite the mantra of Vajrasattva while maintaining this visualization.

DISSOLVING THE VISUALIZATION

WHEN FINISHED, visualize that the Land of Manifest Joy melts into the five Vajrasattvas.

Then the many Vajrasattvas gradually melt from the far reaches into the center of the visualized field and then into your body and the bodies of all sentient beings.

Gradually you and all sentient beings dissolve into light, starting from your extremities and then melting into the *om* at the center of your heart.

This *om* then melts into the *vajra*.

Next, the *vajra* melts into the *ʒa*.

The *ʒa* now melts into the *tva*.

This *tva* melts into the *ʃhabkyu* of the *hum*.

The *ʃhabkyu* melts into the short *a*.

The short *a* melts into the *ha*.

Now the *ha* melts into the circle and crescent on top,
the drop of sun and moon.

The crescent moon then melts into the sun circle.

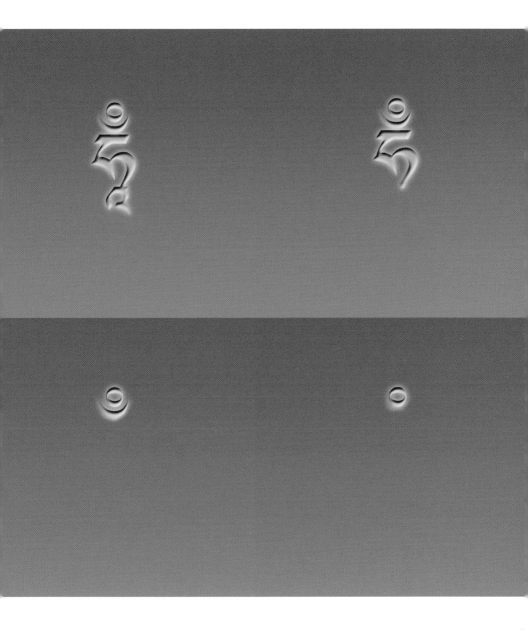

Finally, the sun also melts into the sky like the
disappearance of a rainbow.

Now relax and enter the luminous and empty samadhi,
which is free from concepts and fabrication.
Rest here for as long as you maintain this state of mind.

CONCLUDING

W HEN CONCEPTUAL THOUGHTS again arise, visualize once more that all the material worlds become the land of Vajra-sattva and that all sentient beings transform into the five Vajrasattvas. Then recite the verses for dedication, aspiration, and auspiciousness:

Dedication

May the merit accumulated in this practice and others
be dedicated to all boundless sentient beings.
May all sentient beings soon
reach the attainment of Vajrasattva.

Aspiration

Please purify all the vows that
I and other sentient beings have broken and lost.
May our samaya precepts be kept purely
from now until we obtain enlightenment.

For Auspiciousness

Om
May all appearances be pure and bodies be splendid.
May all sounds perfect the nature of mantra.
May all thoughts ripen into wisdom.
May all merit be perfected and everything auspicious.

PURIFYING
SPECIFIC MISDEEDS
STEP BY STEP

1. PURIFYING THE MISDEED OF SLANDERING THE DHARMA

▸ **Take refuge and generate bodhichitta**

▸ **Reflect on the disadvantages of this negative karma**

The *King of Samadhi Sutra* says:

> The negative karma of destroying all the stupas in Jambudvipa is very heavy, but the negative karma of slandering the sutras is far beyond even that. The negative karma of killing arhats as numerous as the grains of sand in the Ganges River is very heavy, but the negative karma of slandering the sutras exceeds even that.

The *Perfection of Wisdom in Eight Thousand Lines* says, "The negative karma of the five inexpiable misdeeds is not as bad as the negative karma of even a slight slandering of the sutras." It also says:

> Those who slander the Dharma have already abandoned the wisdom of complete enlightenment of the buddhas of the three times and have also abandoned omniscience. Therefore they have destroyed all the Dharma. Due to this negative karma, they will be burned in a hell for

countless years. After being liberated from that hell, they will move to hells in other worlds and again experience the suffering of being burned. When those hells perish, they will yet again go to hells in other worlds and experience the suffering of being burned there. Next they will take rebirth in the region of Yama, in the animal realm, and experience suffering there. Afterward, once they take rebirth as human beings, no matter where they are born, they will be blind, feces cleaners, low caste, bamboo craftsmen, have impaired smell or taste, have deformities of hands or feet, be lepers, have typhus, or be humpbacked, or they will be born where the name of the Three Jewels cannot be heard.

Without purifying the negative karma of slandering the Dharma, there is no chance of taking rebirth in Amitabha's pure land, according to the eighteenth vow of Amitabha in the long *Sukhavativyuha Sutra*:

> May I not obtain complete enlightenment if, when I obtain buddhahood, any sentient beings of the ten directions who hear my name, feel happy, and gain faith cannot be born in my land—so long as they aspire to and dedicate all their virtues toward rebirth in my land after reciting my name for as few as ten times. Excluded, however, are sentient beings who have committed the five inexpiable misdeeds or slandered the Dharma.

▸ **Examine the negative actions you have committed**

Examine whether you have done any of the following:
a. Holding wrong views on or slandering Sutrayana Buddhism
b. Holding wrong views on or slandering Tantrayana Buddhism

c. Thinking some Dharmas are obstacles for obtaining buddhahood and some are the means to obtain buddhahood
d. Grasping and supporting your own school but disliking and slandering other schools
e. Disrespecting some Buddhist schools; criticizing, deprecating, and berating them without understanding their hidden meaning
f. Looking down on or blaspheming any sutras, tantras, or commentaries

Examine whether you have taught others to do the above misdeeds or have rejoiced when you have seen others do them.

▸ **Confess sincerely**

After examination, confess thoroughly in front of a statue or image of Vajrasattva. Even in our degenerate times, a statue or image of Vajrasattva still has the power to save sentient beings, so if you confess in front of his statue or image, Buddha Vajrasattva will surely bestow blessings through his aspiration.

You may not have performed the misdeed of slandering the Dharma in this life, but you have definitely done so from beginningless time, taught others to do so, and rejoiced when others did so. If you do not counteract this, you will fall into the lower realms when that negative karma ripens. Therefore confess all the misdeeds you have accumulated from beginningless time. This same recognition should be applied to all the following misdeeds.

▸ **Take the vow of abstaining from doing this wrong**

Vow with a clear mind:

> From now on, even if my life is endangered, I will never slander, abandon, or damage any Dharma.

Then aspire to protect the Dharma:

> From now on in every life, I will protect and support the Dharma of transmission and the Dharma of realization so that the seed of the Three Jewels ripens endlessly.

▸ **Recite mantras to counteract the negative karma**

Follow the sadhana included in this book. If there is not enough time for the entire practice, you can just recite the hundred-syllable mantra. If this is too difficult, you may just recite the six-syllable mantra. The important thing is to keep in mind the four opponent powers, particularly as related to the misdeed you are focusing on.

▸ **Dedicate the virtues gathered from this process for the benefit of all sentient beings**

2. Purifying the Five Inexpiable Misdeeds

The five inexpiable misdeeds are, with malicious intent, killing one's father, killing one's mother, killing an arhat, causing a schism in a harmonious sangha, and causing a buddha to bleed. The *Vajra Treasure of Patriarchs' Teachings* says that people who kill their parents, khenpos (abbots), or realized acharyas (learned masters) will fall directly into the hells without experiencing the intermediate state. It is said in this commentary that killing one's guru is also an inexpiable misdeed.

▸ **Take refuge and generate bodhichitta**

▸ **Reflect on the disadvantages of this negative karma**

The five inexpiable misdeeds mature in Avichi, the lowest hell. The *Kshitigarbha Ten-Wheel Sutra* says:

> If people commit any of these—the five inexpiable misdeeds, the similar inexpiable misdeeds, the four root misdeeds, slandering the Dharma, or doubting the Three Jewels—then when their bodies perish and their lives end, they will be born in the great hell of Avichi and experience there great suffering without even a moment's respite.

The bodhisattva Kshitigarbha said in the *Kshitigarbha Fundamental Vows Sutra*, "If people are not dutiful to their parents or even kill them, they will fall into the uninterrupted hell and will not get out for hundreds of thousands eons." The same sutra says that Avichi hell is surrounded by an iron wall five hundred kilometers high and nine thousand kilometers around. The fire at the bottom reaches all the way up to the top, and the fire at the top also reaches all the way down to the bottom. Iron snakes and iron dogs disgorge fire and chase the prisoners around the hell and even onto the walls.

There is a bed in this hell that spreads out for five thousand kilometers. No matter how many people suffer on this bed, whether it is hundreds and thousands of beings or just one, they all see their own body covering the entire bed. This is how sentient beings experience the fruit of their karma.

Other prisoners are mauled and dismembered by hundreds of yaksha demons with teeth like swords, eyes like lightning, and copper hands and claws. Some yakshas hold a huge iron halberd and thrust it at the prisoners, sometimes piercing into their nose or mouth, sometimes stabbing into their abdomen or back. Then they throw the prisoners up in the air and either thrust the halberd into their body again when the body falls down or they just let them fall on the bed. Iron eagles peck the prisoners' eyes. Iron snakes twist around the prisoners' neck. Long nails are hammered into the prisoners' joints. Plowshares are furrowed on their tongues. Their intestines are taken out and chopped into pieces. Molten copper is poured into their mouths. Red-hot iron twists around their body. Countless cycles of birth and death of this torture are how they experience their karma. Even after hundreds and thousands of eons, their suffering will not end.

When this world perishes, they will move to another world. When the latter world perishes, they will move to another world. They continue moving to other worlds as the previous ones expire. When the very first world comes into being again, they move back to it, experiencing great suffering endlessly. This is how they experience their karma.

Practice will not succeed, and there is no chance to be born in the Land of Amitabha, if there remains the negative karma of the five inexpiable misdeeds in the mental continuum and no purification is performed. It is said in the *Yogacaryabhumi,* "If people commit the five inexpiable misdeeds and allow the karma to increase, then they will not be able to obtain parinirvana or achieve the arya path in this life."

- **Examine the negative actions you have committed**

Examine whether you have done the five inexpiable misdeeds, taught others to do so, or rejoiced when you have seen others do so.

- **Confess sincerely**

- **Take the vow of abstaining from doing this wrong**

Vow with a clear visualization:

> Even if my life is at stake, I will never commit the five inexpiable misdeeds. I would rather lose my life than break this vow.

- **Recite mantras to counteract the negative karma**

- **Dedicate the merit for the benefit of all sentient beings**

3. Purifying the Five Similar Inexpiable Misdeeds

According to Karma Chakme's *Aspiration to Sukhavati*, the five similar inexpiable misdeeds include killing a monk, killing a novice monk, defiling a nun, damaging stupas, and destroying Dharma halls and the like. Alternate enumerations of these five misdeeds are also found. For example, in the *Abhidharmakosha*, it says:

> Defiling arhat nuns, killing those who have already achieved the path of seeing or the path of learning, robbing the sangha of their food, and destroying Buddha stupas: these are the five similar inexpiable misdeeds.

▸ **Take refuge and generate bodhichitta**

▸ **Reflect on the disadvantages of this negative karma**

The disadvantages of killing monks or novice monks are given in the sutras:

> If a sentient being has a malicious thought toward a monk who wears a monastic robe, this sentient being has already had a malicious thought toward all buddhas of the three times, pratyekabuddhas, and arhats. Since he has a malicious thought toward the noble beings of the three times, the fruits of immeasurable negative karma will mature in him.

The *Buddha Moon Treasure Sutra* (*Fo yuezang jing*) says:

> If people cause one buddha to bleed, they have created inexpiable negative karma and will fall into the uninterrupted hell, so there is no need to mention those who cause

thousands and millions of buddhas to bleed. Nobody is able to say what their karmic fruit will be. However, if somebody harasses, abuses, beats, or ties up those who have taken monastic vows in front of me, or even those who just wear a piece of monastic robe but have not received or observed their precepts, the negative karma of this person is heavier than those who cause buddhas to bleed. Therefore there is no need to mention the negative karma of doing this to a monastic who observes his precepts.

Even observing one item of the precepts has the same great merit as building a stupa, which is an offering field for all humans and gods. Therefore defiling nuns, novice nuns, lay female practitioners, or any female who has taken the eight precepts for one day is damaging Buddhism, and the one who commits this has blocked his way to liberation. In this degenerate time, to hamper people from taking one precept for just one day exceeds the negative karma of preventing people from making offerings for a hundred years.

The disadvantages of destroying statues of the Buddha: Many sutras and tantras have said that it is very meritorious to mold statues of the Buddha, build stupas, and print sutras, and it is also great negative karma to destroy them. The *Lotus Sutra* says, "The Buddha has manifested in different appearances to facilitate sentient beings' virtuous deeds." Statues of the Buddha are the craft nirmanakaya—one of the four types of nirmanakaya—and sutras are the relics of Buddha's dharmakaya. Therefore it creates extremely negative karma to destroy sutras and statues. Even to sell statues or sutras creates negative karma. Profit made through this kind of business can only be used for propagating and preserving Dharma.

The negative karmic results of destroying stupas: Stupas are a vessel for the Buddha's mind, so it creates boundless merit to build stupas and infinite disadvantages to destroy them.

The negative karmic results of destroying Dharma halls: Dharma halls are a vessel for the Three Jewels where the sangha can assemble. Even to sleep, spit, blow your nose, leave tea dregs, or break wind in them will cause you to fall into the lower realms, so there is no need to mention the results of destroying them. Stealing the materials intended for building a hall or for other edifices of the Three Jewels, which then results in the planned hall being reduced in size, is the same negative karma as destroying the halls.

▸ **Examine the negative actions you have committed**

Check if you have done any of the following negative actions:
a. Killing monks or novice monks
b. Harassing, abusing, or tying up nuns or novice nuns
c. Disrespecting or damaging monastic robes
d. Damaging female practitioners' precepts or creating unfavorable conditions for them to observe their precepts
e. Destroying or selling Buddhist scriptures and statues, or blaspheming, slandering, or disrespecting scriptures and statues
f. Destroying or making irresponsible remarks about stupas or showing disrespect in front of stupas
g. Destroying sutra halls or sleeping, spitting, blowing your nose, leaving tea dregs, or breaking wind in sutra halls
h. Sitting on a dirty cushion in sutra halls
i. Destroying the halls, Dharma thrones, or offering containers of the Three Jewels
j. Being part of an occupying force of the land of the Three Jewels

Have you ever taught others to commit the above negative actions or rejoiced when you have seen others do so? This also counts as performing the actions.

▸ **Confess sincerely**

▸ **Take the vow of abstaining from doing this wrong**

Vow with a clear mind:

> From now on, I will never kill any monk, novice monk, or
> defile any nun who observes precepts. I will never harass,
> abuse, disrespect, or blaspheme them either. I will never
> destroy any stupas or Dharma halls. I will watch my mind
> so as not to have any disrespectful thought toward any of
> them. Even if my life is endangered, I will not abandon
> this vow.

Also take the vow:

> I will respect all monks and novice monks of the Buddha,
> even those who just appear to be monks. I will respect all
> Buddhist stupas, statues, halls, and sutras as if they are
> the real Three Jewels.

▸ **Recite mantras to counteract the negative karma**

▸ **Dedicate the merit**

4. Purifying the Misdeed of Killing

▶ **Take refuge and generate bodhichitta**

▶ **Reflect on the disadvantages of this negative karma**

Whether out of hatred or attachment, with a strong emotion or a weak one, he who kills a sentient being will be born in the three lower realms and suffer there for 200 billion years. This is the direct effect of that act.

After leaving the lower realms, no matter where this person is born, he will be avenged five hundred lives over, experience a short life span, and have many diseases due to his previous fault of killing. This is the causally concordant experiencing effect.

This person will be born as a bloodthirsty animal, such as an eagle or wolf. Even as a human, he will become a butcher. This is the causally concordant habitual effect.

If someone causes others to lose their power and stature, then the result is that this person will become powerless, have no stature, and be a very weak, lowly person. The environmental effect is that the place where this wrongdoer takes rebirth will be infertile and always threatened by plague, violence, and theft.

▶ **Examine the negative actions you have committed**

Check whether you have done any of the following negative actions:
  a. Killing people or human fetuses
  b. Cooking living creatures inappropriately and causing them extreme suffering
  c. Fishing, shooting birds, filling burrows, covering dens, breaking eggs, damaging fetuses, waking up hibernating creatures

Check whether you have done any of the following unkind actions:
  a. Not saving a living creature when it is being killed

b. Feeling no compassion when you see human beings or animals die
c. Treating livestock too harshly; even when they are exhausted, still using or thrashing them without mercy
d. Cheating or making fun of the blind, the deaf, the sick, the mentally handicapped, the aged, or children
e. Keeping poultry in cages or tying up livestock
f. Not helping widowers, widows, poor people, and people who need food, drink, or clothing
g. Rejoicing when you watch violent movies or war reports

Have you ever taught others to commit the above negative actions or rejoiced when you have seen others do so?

▸ **Confess sincerely**

▸ **Take the vow of abstaining from doing this wrong**

Make the following vows with a clear mind:

> From now on, I will never kill any sentient beings. I will not kill any big animals such as lions. I will never kill any livestock such as pigs, horses, cows, or goats. I will never kill mosquitoes, flies, fleas, lice, and so on. To further demonstrate my resolve, I vow to not even kill very rare or mythical beings, like dragons. Even if my life is endangered, I will not abandon this vow.

To reinforce this vow, visualize that you will not kill any sentient beings even when somebody threatens or tortures you. Even better, make the commitment that you will not do anything that will hurt or insult sentient beings through your body, speech, and mind. Finally, resolve:

From now on, I will benefit, save, and protect all sentient beings.

▶ Recite mantras to counteract the negative karma

▶ Dedicate the merit

5. Purifying the Misdeed of Taking What Has Not Been Given

▸ **Take refuge and generate bodhichitta**

▸ **Reflect on the disadvantages of this negative karma**

The direct effect is that the thief will be born in one of the three lower realms, determined by the strength of the motivation.

The causally concordant experiencing effect is that when they take rebirth in human form, they will be born as beggars and slaves. If they have little wealth, it will be extorted by the strong, robbed by the weak, or just lost, diminished, or destroyed. They have no right to use their wealth as they wish but have to share their wealth with gods, humans, and spirits. In addition, their food has no nutrition; their crops will be destroyed by drought, frost, hail, or pests.

The causally concordant habitual effect is that they are fond of stealing and cheating in business life after life. When they take rebirth as animals, they will become mice or dogs who are fond of stealing.

In particular, people who steal even a small amount of wealth intended for making offerings, molding statues of the Buddha, building stupas, or printing sutras will surely fall into the cold hells or the hungry ghost realm. Stealing as little as a needle tip of the wealth of the Three Jewels brings a fall into the lower realms.

This environmental effect will be to take rebirth in barren regions where famine is frequent.

The disadvantages of stealing the wealth of the Three Jewels, one's guru, or one's parents
The *Samadhi of Visualizing the Buddha Sutra* (*Buddhanusmriti Samadhi Sagara Sutra*) says, "The wrong of stealing Sangha property exceeds the wrong of killing 84,000 parents." The *Trove of Precious Jewels Sutra* (*Ratnarashi Sutra*) concurs, "You should rather eat your body's flesh

than misuse the properties of the Three Jewels." The *Flower Ornament Sutra* (*Avatamsaka Sutra*) even goes so far as to say, "I can save those who have committed the five inexpiable misdeeds and the four fundamental misdeeds, but I cannot save those who steal the property of the Sangha." The *Excellent Teaching on the Foundations of Mindfulness Sutra* (*Saddharma Smrityupasthana Sutra*) states:

> The negative karma of stealing even a little from the Buddha, Dharma, and Sangha is heavy and huge. If people steal property, such as the Dharma or statues, from the Buddha and Dharma but they later return it in full, then their negative karma is purified. If they steal from the Sangha, however, then until the Sangha accepts what they return, their negative karma will not be purified, because this misdeed is very severe. If they steal food, they will fall into the great hell; if it is not food, they will be born somewhere in between the hells, in Avichi hell, or in the neighboring hells where it is extremely dark.

To steal even one needle from the Three Jewels or from one's parents will make one fall into Avichi hell. If monks or novice monks take five grams of silver from the common property of the Sangha, they will violate as many grave offenses as the number of the Sangha members robbed.

▸ **Examine the negative actions you have committed**

Check whether you have ever done any of the following:
  a. Taking, without being given, the property belonging to the Three Jewels, your guru, your parents, your country, or other people
  b. Not compensating after damaging the property belonging to the Three Jewels, your guru, your parents, your country, or other people

c. Not paying back funds you borrowed from the Three Jewels, your guru, your parents, your country, or other people
d. Engaging in tax evasion, obtaining wealth by power or deception, or seeking huge profit with little investment
e. Appropriating public funds for personal use
f. Not using money according to its appropriate purpose

Check whether you have ever taught others to commit the above negative actions or have rejoiced when you have seen others do so.

▸ **Confess sincerely**

▸ **Take the vow of abstaining from doing this wrong**

Vow with a clear mind:

> From now on, I will never take anything without it being given. I will not steal or obtain things through deception or force. I will never steal anything from the Three Jewels, gurus, or my parents. I will never take anything belonging to others. Even if my life is endangered, I will not break this vow.

To reinforce this vow, visualize that even if you are dying because of hunger and cold, you will not steal anything. Also promise to abstain from cherishing the property of others. Then take this vow:

> From now on, I will make offerings to those superior and give charity to those less fortunate; I will make offerings to the guru and the Three Jewels and benefit all sentient beings.

▸ **Recite mantras to counteract the negative karma**

▸ **Dedicate the merit**

6. Purifying the Misdeed of Sexual Misconduct

▸ **Take refuge and generate bodhichitta**

▸ **Reflect on the disadvantages of this negative karma**

The direct effect varies according to the strength of the motivation driving the sexual misconduct. In any case, those who commit this misdeed will be born in the three lower realms. Heavy wrongdoers will take rebirth in the Hill of Iron Shalmali Trees hell, in dirty mud, or as parasites in a woman's uterus.

If the wrongdoer is reborn as a man, he will experience the suffering of being robbed of his wife by force or being discontented with his wife. His wife will steal and have a bad temper. They will always fight like enemies. Nowadays, we see many families that are unhappy, couples fighting day and night and having to get divorced or live separately. These are all the causally concordant fruits of sexual misconduct in past lives.

The causally concordant habitual effects are that those who have done this misdeed will be insatiable with respect to mating and fond of sexual misconduct, or born as an animal with strong sexual desire, such as a rooster.

The *Grove of Pearls in the Garden of the Dharma* (*Fayuan zhulin*) says:

> The Buddha says that there are ten negative effects of sexual misconduct: The first is fear of being killed by your lover's spouse. The second is discord with your own spouse. The third is that your negative karma increases and positive karma decreases. The fourth is that your spouse and children are lonely. The fifth is that your wealth wanes quickly. The sixth is that people always suspect you of malicious behavior. The seventh is that your relatives and friends slander you. The eighth is that

you will make enemies widely. The ninth is that you will be born in a hell. The tenth is that when you finally obtain a male human body after you have finished suffering in the hells, your wife will not be chaste. After suffering that with the male body, you will obtain a female human body, but you will have to share your husband with others.

▸ **Examine the negative actions you have committed**

Examine whether you have ever done the following:
  a. Had sex with an inappropriate partner, inappropriate body parts, at the inappropriate time, or in inappropriate places
  b. Wished to have sex with a prostitute
  c. Had an extramarital affair
  d. Wanted to possess somebody who looked attractive to you
  e. Watched or disseminated obscene publications, pictures, and movies
  f. Promoted sexual desire and sex
  g. Viewed or listened to erotic scenes
  h. Performed masturbation or visualized having sex
  i. Had sex while an ordained member of the Buddhist sangha

Have you ever taught others to commit the above negative actions or rejoiced when you have seen others do so?

▸ **Confess sincerely**

▸ **Take the vow of abstaining from doing this wrong**

Vow with a clear mind:

> From now on, I will never commit any sexual misconduct. No matter the age or social status of the person I meet, I will protect my chastity like jade.

To reinforce this vow, visualize that someone beautiful is in front of you, and then think, "I will not violate this vow even if my life is endangered. I will watch and protect my mind and thought." Then take this vow:

> I will praise the merit of the discipline of celibacy and guide all sentient beings away from sexual desire so that they may obtain a pure and cool mind.

▶ **Recite mantras to counteract the negative karma**

▶ **Dedicate the merit**

7. Purifying the Misdeed of Lying

▸ **Take refuge and generate bodhichitta**

▸ **Reflect on the disadvantages of this negative karma**

The direct effect is that the liars fall into different lower realms depending on the motivation.

The causally concordant effects are that when they take rebirth as human beings, their words will not be trusted even by their parents. Even if they want to tell the truth, it turns out to be a lie. They have stale-smelling breath. They are inarticulate and tongue-tied. Wherever they go, they always encounter beguilers cheating them. Whatever they do is in vain. They like to tell lies life after life. In particular, those who say they don't see when they actually do will be born blind.

The *Mahaprajnaparamita Shastra* (*Dazhidu lun*) says:

> As the Buddha says, there are ten negative effects of lying. What are they? The first is they will have bad breath. The second is that good gods will keep away from them and nonhumans will draw close to harm them. The third is that when they tell the truth, nobody will believe them. The fourth is that when the wise are conversing, they will be unable to attend. The fifth is that they will always be slandered and their infamy will spread everywhere. The sixth is that nobody will respect them and, when they give a command, nobody will perform it. The seventh is that they will always be unhappy. The eighth is that they plant the seed for the causally concordant habitual fruit of slandering others. The ninth is that when they die, they will fall into a hell. The tenth is that when they are born as humans again, they will always be slandered.

It says in the Vinaya:

> Liars are like the water that remains in a container after it is emptied; their merit is tiny. Like a small drop of water that leaks on the ground, their merit of celibacy will leak out. Like an empty container turned upside down, their merit of celibacy and other behaviors will be a thorough defeat. Like a crazy elephant doing everything, the foolish liar will say anything.

The *Essential Meditation Techniques Sutra* (*Chan miyaofa jing*) says:

> For the sake of gain and interest, some people among the fourfold disciples—monks, nuns, and male and female lay practitioners—may insatiably cheat others with nonvirtuous deeds. Some may, for the sake of gain and fame, tell others they are meditating when they are not meditating, nor even paying attention to the action of their body, speech, and mind; and thus they commit one of the grave offenses, which hinders the virtuous path. If they do not tell the truth nor regret such offense, then after a short period of time, they will [commit a serious violation]. If this violation lasts for one to two days, they will become thieves in god and human realms, or the killer of demons, and they will certainly fall into the lower realms and commit the most grave offenses....
>
> If someone lies to people, saying that he has accomplished the meditation on uncleanness or the highest accomplishment, then at the time of death, this liar will fall into the lowest hell, Avichi, as quickly as lightning and stay there for one eon. After getting out of that hell, this liar will be born as a hungry ghost and live for eight thousand years eating red-hot iron pills. After that, such a liar

will be born in the animal realm with constant burdens. At each death, the liar's skin will be peeled off. After five hundred lives, such a liar will finally have a chance to be born as a human being, but this person will be deaf, blind, and dumb and have all kinds of disease. The suffering this person will experience is indescribable.

► **Examine the negative actions you have committed**

Examine whether you have done any of the following:
  a. Telling people you have seen buddhas, bodhisattvas, spirits, and gods when you have not
  b. Telling people you have obtained realization and prophecy when you have not
  c. Telling people you have mastered the meaning of the Dharma when you have not
  d. Slandering the Dharma, gurus, and Sangha without reason
  e. Lying to gurus or parents
  f. Telling others you possess merit that you do not and thus cheating followers in order to gain fame, property, and other advantages
  g. Telling lies for reputation and profit when doing business

Check whether you have ever taught others to commit the above negative actions or rejoiced when you have seen others do so.

► **Confess sincerely**

► **Take the vow of abstaining from doing this wrong**

Vow with a clear visualization:

> From now on, I will never tell lies and never tell others that I have obtained what I have not or realized what I have not. I will never slander or cheat the fields of great

power: my gurus, the Three Jewels, or my parents. I will not lie to any sentient being. Even if my life is in danger, I will not break this vow.

To reinforce this vow, visualize that you will not tell lies even when you are tortured or enticed with billions of dollars. Then take this vow:

I will tell the truth at all times and in all places.

▸ **Recite mantras to counteract the negative karma**

▸ **Dedicate the merit**

8. Purifying the Misdeed of Divisive Speech

▸ Take refuge and generate bodhichitta

▸ Reflect on the disadvantages of this negative karma

People who create the negative karma of divisive speech will fall into the three lower realms: suffering a long eon in the Torn Tongues hell, where the tongue is plucked out again and again and they are forced to drink molten copper; or suffering as animals that eat feces and dirt or as something that does not have a tongue, such as a crab or lobster. These are the direct effects.

The causally concordant effects are that even when they become human beings, they do not have a tongue and always have bad breath. Their voice is unpleasant, unclear, or even mute. Their teeth are not white or level. When they say something good, others will not trust or use their idea. Because of the effects of their remaining karma, their dependents' minds are unstable, and they are wicked, disharmonious, and refuse to live together.

The causally concordant habitual effect is that they are fond of divisive speech. Lakla Sönam Chödup's great commentary on the *Aspiration to Sukhavati* says:

> As is said in the *Manjushri Root Tantra*, "The one who creates conflict in a monastery and among gurus is like a stick stirring blood. After his death, he will immediately be born in Avichi hell..." If a Sangha is provoked into conflict, all sentient beings in that area will become angry until the situation abates, and so they all will be born in a hell because of their anger. Just as seeds cannot germinate on burned land, practicing the Dharma within several leagues of a community involved in a conflict will not bear fruit.

▶ Examine the negative actions you have committed

Examine whether you have ever done any of the following:
  a. Sowing discord among gurus, great masters, and their followers
  b. Spoiling harmony among Buddhist organizations
  c. Spoiling harmony among Buddhist practitioners
  d. Sowing discord among people related by blood
  e. Breaking others' marriages
  f. Sowing discord among colleagues, friends, neighbors, house-masters and servants, or teachers and students

Check whether you have ever taught others to commit the above negative actions or rejoiced when you have seen others do so.

▶ Confess sincerely

▶ Take the vow of abstaining from doing this wrong

Vow with a clear visualization:

> In the future, I will never utter divisive speech to gurus, great masters, or Buddhist friends. I will never say divisive words to any organization or individual. Furthermore, I will never sow discord among any sentient beings and will not even let such thoughts arise. Even if my life is endangered, I will not give up my vow.

Then take this vow:

> I will say harmonious words at all times and in all places. I will try my best to reconcile broken relationships.

▶ Recite mantras to counteract the negative karma

▶ Dedicate the merit

9. PURIFYING THE MISDEED OF HARSH SPEECH

▸ **Take refuge and generate bodhichitta**

▸ **Reflect on the disadvantages of this negative karma**

The direct effect is that the speaker will fall into the three lower realms. Even when they become human beings, they never hear pleasant words. They always feel fretful and scorned by others. They are always anxious, like wild animals. They never feel comfortable in their heart and always encounter unscrupulous friends. They are always born in adverse places and speak harshly life after life.

Those who criticize Buddha statues and stupas will especially experience the fruit of this negative karma.

Whatever pejorative you call others you will experience yourself five hundred times over. If you use an insulting name for a monk, novice monk, and so forth, the effect is to fall into a hell.

As it is said in the *Chapter on Causality* (*Yinyuan pin*), "Being born to speak malicious words when they open their mouth, they are like a sharp ax that chops itself." Padmasambhava has said, "Evil people's words are like a poisonous tree; whatever part of the tree is touched breaks." It is said in a sutra, "Overwhelmed by the defilement of harsh speech, anybody who talks harshly will have no happiness and peace. People who say harsh words are as fierce and cruel as lions and snakes; they have no chance to take birth in the higher realms." The *Repaying Kindness Sutra* (*Da fangbian baoan jing*) says:

> A broiling iron wheel is always spinning above their heads, so their suffering is unbearable. [If one says harsh words, the fruit of this negative karma is even more unbearable.] Therefore never say harsh words.

▶ **Examine the negative actions you have committed**

Examine whether you have ever done the following:
  a. Speaking harshly to a guru, the Three Jewels, the elders, parents, peers, or those who are younger or inferior to you
  b. Saying immoral words
  c. Spreading news of others' evil deeds
  d. Insulting others
  e. Deliberately picking on the shortcomings of a worthy person from the past
  f. Speaking harshly after getting angry during a debate
  g. Criticizing Buddha statues and stupas

Check whether you have ever taught others to commit the above negative actions or rejoiced when you have seen others do so.

▶ **Confess sincerely**

▶ **Take the vow of abstaining from doing this wrong**

Vow with a clear visualization:

> In the future, I will never say harsh words. I will not say harsh words to my guru, the Three Jewels, my parents, or elders. I will not say harsh words to Buddhist friends, colleagues, children, or inferiors. I will not even say harsh words to animals. Even if my life is endangered, I will not give up my vow.

Aspire to say pleasant words to all sentient beings.

▶ **Recite mantras to counteract the negative karma**

▶ **Dedicate the merit**

10. Purifying the Misdeed of Worthless Chatter

▸ **Take refuge and generate bodhichitta**

▸ **Reflect on the disadvantages of this negative karma**

The direct effect of engaging in worthless chatter is to be born in the three lower realms. Afterward, as human beings once again, everybody dislikes you. You talk endlessly and incoherently and always feel anxious. Nobody trusts what you say. You are fond of worthless talk life after life.

Worthless chatter undermines the merit of chanting. Padmasambhava said, "One month of chanting punctuated by senseless chatter is not as meritorious as chanting without interruption for just one day."

The *Grove of Pearls in the Garden of the Dharma* says:

> Because of worthless speech, there is illusion. Because of illusion, there is negative karma. Because of negative karma, there is suffering. Therefore, in order to obtain the state of the noble beings and the truth, we must tell the truth. If we speak illusorily, it will only become falsehood.

▸ **Examine the negative actions you have committed**

Check whether you have ever committed the following through your speech:

    a. Encouraging fights, litigation, and competition
    b. Being fond of senseless talk
    c. Being fond of chanting non-Buddhist scriptures and mantras
    d. Being fond of talking about rulers, politicians, and bandits in public
    e. Talking about pranks, entertainment, and sexual desire
    f. Speaking drunk or crazy words

g. Speaking for wrong livelihoods, such as receiving offerings or funds through cheating, flattery, and so forth

h. Intermixing mundane words while chanting sutras and mantras

Check whether you have ever taught others to commit the above negative actions or rejoiced when you have seen others do so.

▸ **Confess sincerely**

▸ **Take the vow of abstaining from doing this wrong**

Vow with a clear visualization:

> From now on, I will never speak of warfare or competition or use senseless words. I will never talk about pranks, entertainment, or sexual desires. I will never talk about rulers, politicians, or bandits. I will not read or chant non-Buddhist scriptures, which can engender attachment or anger. Even if my life is endangered, I will not give up this vow. I will aspire to speak meaningful words with mindfulness and awareness.

▸ **Recite mantras to counteract the negative karma**

▸ **Dedicate the merit**

11. Purifying the Misdeed of Covetousness

- ▸ Take refuge and generate bodhichitta

- ▸ Reflect on the disadvantages of this negative karma

The direct effect of covetousness is to be born in the three lower realms. Afterward, as a human again, you will be ugly and very poor. Even when you obtain some wealth, it will be quickly depleted. Because of the obstacle of covetousness, none of your wishes will be fulfilled. You will always be born in an adverse environment and continue to be covetous.

- ▸ Examine the negative actions you have committed

Check whether you have ever had the following thoughts:
  a. The thought of owning the property of others
  b. Longing for offerings and servants
  c. Longing for respect from others
  d. Longing for fame and resources
  e. The thought of showing off your merit or longing for a good reputation
  f. Longing for the sensual enjoyment of the god realm
  g. Longing for power and a high position

- ▸ Confess sincerely

- ▸ Take the vow of abstaining from doing this wrong

Take this vow with a clear visualization:

> In the future, no matter in what circumstances I find myself, I will watch my mind to prevent any desire for wealth, fame, or respect. Even if my life is endangered, I

will not give up this vow. I aspire to be content with what I have.

▸ **Recite mantras to counteract the negative karma**

▸ **Dedicate the merit**

12. Purifying the Misdeed of Hatred

▸ **Take refuge and generate bodhichitta**

▸ **Reflect on the disadvantages of this negative karma**

When the effect of harmful thoughts ripens, those who had these thoughts will fall into the three lower realms. Afterward, if they are lucky enough to be born as human beings, they will be ugly, foolish, and ignorant. They will always suffer from physical and mental pains and be subject to endless bullying and humiliation. They will be born in places that are frightful, empty, obscure, and barbaric, or where death is sudden due to frequent fighting and wars. They will bear malicious thoughts life after life and not have the chance for loving-kindness to arise.

▸ **Examine the negative actions you have committed**

Check whether you have ever had the following harmful thoughts:
   a. Thinking how to kill others or tie them up
   b. Wishing that the wealth of others wanes spontaneously or by some cause
   c. Contemplating revenge after recalling the harm others are doing or have done to you
   d. Wishing others to lose close relatives in this life
   e. Wishing others to lose property in this life
   f. Wishing others to be unsuccessful in their undertakings and not famous
   g. Wishing others to lose their motivation or opportunity for virtuous listening, reflecting, and meditating
   h. Rejoicing when you see others meet with misfortune
   i. Wishing other people's relatives and friends to decline
   j. Wishing others to be reborn in a lower realm in a future life

▸ **Confess sincerely**

▸ **Take the vow of abstaining from doing this wrong**

Vow with a clear visualization:

> From now on, I will never bear harmful thoughts toward
> any sentient beings, not even ants or mosquitoes. Even
> if my life is endangered, I will not abandon this vow. I
> aspire to raise the mind of loving-kindness toward all sen-
> tient beings and perform only nonharmful acts.

▸ **Recite mantras to counteract the negative karma**

▸ **Dedicate the merit**

13. Purifying the Misdeed of Holding Wrong Views

▸ **Take refuge and generate bodhichitta**

▸ **Reflect on the disadvantages of this negative karma**

The direct effect of holding wrong views is to be born in the lower three realms in accordance with the motivation for the wrong view. Those with the worst motivation are born in Avichi hell, where they will experience all the sufferings in all the other hells and then be born as animals. Even if a human body is obtained later, it will be wasted due to the causally concordant effects of their previous nonvirtue. They will be born as wrong-view holders life after life, the disadvantages of which are indescribable. Even their virtuous roots will turn into the cause of their suffering. As the bodhisattva Nagarjuna said, "He who wants to be born in the higher realms should cultivate right view; even if a wrong-view holder practices virtues, the effect will still be unbearable."

Words of My Perfect Teacher says:

> To have wrong views, even for an instant, is to break all your vows and to cut yourself off from the Buddhist community. It also negates the freedom in this human existence to practice the Dharma. From the moment your mind is defiled by false views, even the good you do no longer leads to liberation and the harm you do can no longer be confessed.[15]

The *Mahaprajnaparamita Shastra* says:

> The negative karma of holding wrong views is very heavy, so even the positive karma of observing precepts through body and speech will be defiled by the nonvirtuous mind

of wrong views. As the Buddha himself said, when the bitter seeds are sowed, though the fruits are formed by the four great elements, the bitter taste will still remain. Likewise, no matter how well the wrong-view holders observe precepts and how diligently they practice, all their actions will become nonvirtuous.

▸ **Examine the negative actions you have committed**

Check whether you have ever maintained the following wrong views:

    a. Believing there is no past or future life
    b. Believing there is no cause and effect, and believing that practicing virtue has no merit and that committing nonvirtues causes no negative consequences
    c. Believing the Three Jewels do not exist
    d. Believing no pure land exists

▸ **Confess sincerely**

▸ **Take the vow of abstaining from doing this wrong**

Vow with a clear visualization:

> From now on, I will never hold wrong views about the Three Jewels or about the law of cause and effect. Even if my life is endangered, I will not abandon this vow. Therefore I aspire to encourage all sentient beings to cultivate the right view of cause and effect and so forth.

▸ **Recite mantras to counteract the negative karma**

▸ **Dedicate the merit**

14. Purifying Powerful and Heavy Misdeeds

▸ **Take refuge and generate bodhichitta**

▸ **Reflect on the disadvantages of the negative karma**

The defects of negative karma with the Three Jewels as the ozbject
The *Sun Essence Sutra* (*Suryagarbha Sutra*) says that if those who have broken their precepts use even a little of the property belonging to the Sangha, such as a piece of leaf, a flower, or a fruit, they will be born in a hell. When they leave that hell after an extremely long time, they will be born as animals without feet or hands in corpse fields or as blind and hungry ghosts without feet or hands and thus suffer for many years.

The *Seal of Engagement in Kindling the Power of Faith Sutra* (*Shraddha-baladhanavataramudra Sutra*) says:

> If out of hatred one person locks up all the sentient beings of the ten directions in a dark prison and if another person turns his back to a bodhisattva and does not want to see the bodhisattva, the latter has created immeasurably more negative karma than the former. If one person robs sentient beings of all of their property and another person slanders a bodhisattva, the latter has created immeasurably more negative karma than the former. If one person destroys as many stupas as the number of the grains of sand in the Ganges River and another one bears a malicious thought toward, gets angry at, and hurls bad words at a Mahayana bodhisattva who has gained the supreme determination, the latter also has created immeasurably more negative karma than the former.

Shantideva's *Guide to the Bodhisattva's Way of Life* says:

One who has malicious thoughts toward a bodhisattva,
  who is practicing the greatest generosity,
the Buddha says that this person will fall into a hell
for as many eons as the moments his malicious thought
  lasts.

Enacting the Punishment of Breaking Precepts Sutra (*Dushilanigraha Sutra*) says:

> Compared to a worldly person who commits the ten non-virtues and continuously accumulates much negative karma for a hundred years, a monk who has broken his precepts and yet wears a robe and takes offerings from Buddhist believers for just one day and one night collects far more negative karma. This nonvirtue has a very strong power due to the object of this negative karma.

The *Trove of Precious Jewels Sutra* says:

> If monastics give little attention to the precepts, do not respect their robes, keep head and facial hair, and wear cosmetics, they will be born in the lonely hell after death. They will keep their appearance as a monastic in hell and suffer being burned in the three robes, offering bowls, and cushions.

The *King of Samadhi Sutra* says, "If monastics hate each other, they cannot be saved by their precepts, studying, concentration, staying in solitude, or making offerings to the Buddha."

The defects of the negative karma committed with gurus as the objects

The kindness of the khenpo masters who transmit the precepts of the three vehicles is beyond that of all buddhas. Bearing wrong views or malicious thoughts toward them for even a single moment guarantees birth in a hell. Even just having a flickering conceptual thought of superiority to the guru, or disrespecting a master who gives a literal explanation, or a guru who gives a transmission of a four-lined verse, the defects will be very heavy.

The *Kalachakra Tantra* says, "How many moments a Vajrayana disciple bears malicious thoughts toward his vajra guru, then that many great eons this disciple will stay in the vajra hell."

It is said in the tantra, "If you do not regard those who teach you even one verse of Dharma as your teacher, then you will be born as a dog for a hundred lives and afterward become a human being with birthmarks." "After relying on a guru, no matter whether the guru is good or bad, the disciple should not violate the guru's instruction. If the disciple breaks this rule, he will be born in the vajra hell." "Even if the guru has no merit, after relying on him, if the disciple abandons, humiliates, or slanders him, his negative karma is indescribable."

The negative karma committed with parents as the objects

The *Contemplation of the Mind Ground Sutra (Xindiguan jing)* says:

> Fathers have the kindness of love; mothers have the kindness of compassion. Their kindness for nurturing us is as vast as the universe; their compassion is incomparably wide and immense. Mount Meru is the highest point in the world, but the kindness of the compassionate mother transcends even it. The earth is the heaviest thing in the universe, but the kindness of the compassionate mother is also beyond it. If children turn away from or are not

filial to their parents and make their parents curse due to resentment, then the children will be born in the three lower realms. The fastest thing in the world is the hurricane, but the maturation of a parent's resentment is even faster.

▶ **Examine the negative actions you have committed**

Check whether you have ever done the following:

a. Using the Sangha's property when your precepts are broken
b. Using property that has already been offered to the Sangha or giving it to laypeople
c. Receiving offerings when your precepts are broken
d. Receiving offerings but paying little attention to your precepts
e. Bearing hatred toward Buddhist friends
f. Bearing hatred, aversion, or unpleasant thoughts toward a bodhisattva
g. Slandering or insulting a bodhisattva
h. Hindering a bodhisattva's virtuous deeds
i. Disrespecting gurus by bearing bad thoughts such as thinking you are superior to them
j. Saying disrespectful words to gurus and mentioning their faults
k. Disrespecting gurus by not supporting or waiting upon them
l. Disobeying, not following, or not paying attention to your gurus' instruction
m. Holding wrong views toward gurus
n. Hindering the activities and virtuous deeds of gurus
o. Abandoning gurus
p. Not respecting or supporting parents
q. Disobeying the reasonable admonitions of parents
r. Being angry at or clashing with parents after being scolded by them

s. Not wisely dissuading parents from bad behavior

t. Not making offerings to the Sangha for the Buddhist rituals that will liberate your parents from the lower realms after they die

Check whether you have ever taught others to commit the above negative actions or rejoiced when you have seen others do so.

▸ **Confess sincerely**

▸ **Take the vow of abstaining from doing this wrong**

Vow with a clear visualization:

> From now on, I would rather give up my life than harm, disrespect, slander, be angry at, or abandon any of the fields of great power such as my guru, the Three Jewels, bodhisattvas, or my parents.

Aspire to respect gurus, bodhisattvas, and Buddhist friends and to be dutiful to your parents. Then visualize and think, "Since I have already renounced wordly life (or been ordained) and received precepts, I should practice day and night and never receive offerings if I am not qualified to receive them."

▸ **Recite mantras to counteract the negative karma**

▸ **Dedicate the merit**

CONCLUSION

Even though the effects of committing all these negative actions is heavy and can lead to intolerable suffering, the power of Vajrasattva meditation, when performed sincerely and with a devout and steady mind, can counteract even the heaviest of misdeeds. Our gurus have been so kind in showing us this method. With tears in our eyes, our gratitude to them for liberating us from our past and showing the pure path to peerless happiness for both ourselves and others is boundless. We can never repay such kindness. But we can dedicate the merit of this practice to perfect buddhahood for the benefit of sentient beings everywhere. May the merit from these visualizations, prayers, and pure intentions become the cause to completely empty the lower realms and bring peace to the minds of each and every one of our kind mothers.

NOTES

1. Patrul Rinpoche, *Words of My Perfect Teacher* (Boston: Shambhala, 1998), 263–64.
2. *Sangs rgyas thams cad kyi dgongs pa 'dus pa'i mdo*, one of the principal anuyoga tantras of the Dzokchen tradition.
3. These five misdeeds are drawing blood from a buddha, killing an arhat, killing one's mother, killing one's father, and creating a schism in the spiritual community.
4. Patrul, *Words*, 279.
5. *Dri med bshags pa'i rgyud*, a.k.a. *Stainless King of Confessions* (*Dri ma med pa'i rgyal po*).
6. *Vajrapanjaratantra* (*Rdo rje gur zhes bya ba'i rgyud*).
7. Patrul, *Words*, 264–65.
8. Modified from translation by Judith Hanson in Jamgon Kongtrul, *The Torch of Certainty* (Boston: Shambhala, 1977), 86–87. Kongtrul cites it simply as from an Indian text.
9. Patrul, *Words*, 280.
10. Patrul, *Words*, 276.
11. The five buddha bodies are the nirmanakaya, sambhogakaya, and dharmakaya along with the essence body (*svabhavikakaya*) and the utterly pure essence body. The five wisdoms are mirror-like wisdom, the wisdom of equality, discriminating wisdom, accomplishing wisdom, and wisdom of the dharmadhatu.
12. These buddhas occupy a central role in tantric Buddhism, with one pair in the center and one in each of the four cardinal directions—the buddhas Vairochana, Akshobhya, Ratnasambhava, Amitabha, and Amoghasiddhi in union with their respective consorts Akashadhatvishvari, Lochana, Mamaki, Pandaravasini, and Samayatara.

13. The three kinds of sufferings are the suffering of suffering, the suffering of change, and the pervasive suffering of conditioned existence. The eight kinds of suffering are the sufferings of birth, old age, sickness, death, the fear of meeting enemies, fear of losing loved ones, not getting what we want, and encountering what we don't want.

14. A *vidyadhara*, or "knowledge holder," is a tantric master who abides in a state of realization. The four levels of vidyadharas are the matured vidyadhara, the vidyadhara with mastery over life, the mahamudra vidyadhara, and the spontaneously accomplished vidyadhara.

15. Patrul, *Words*, 112.

ABOUT JIGME PHUNTSOK RINPOCHE

Dharma King Jigme Phuntsok Rinpoche, the composer of the Vajrasattva liturgy in this book, was born in 1933 in Padma, in the Dhok region of Kham, now part of Qinghai province. It is said he was born with his head up and immediately sat cross-legged with his back straight before reciting seven times the mantra of Manjushri, the bodhisattva of wisdom, *Om arapachana dhih.* He was subsequently recognized by many great masters of the time as an incarnation of the eminent treasure revealer Lerab Lingpa (1856–1926). According to the terma *Dharmadhatu Vajra*, his other incarnations include the Indian arhat Sagilha, famed for writing the *Flower Garland*; Guru Rinpoche's twenty-fourth disciple, Dorje Dudjom; Sakya Pandita Kunga Gyaltsen (1147–1216); Khedrup

Norsang Gyatso (1423–1513), a student of the first Dalai Lama and guru to the second; Minyak Kunsang Sönam (1823–1905), composer of a highly regarded commentary on the *Guide to the Bodhisattva Way of Life*; and many others.

When he was three or four years old, he already had such profound faith in the nineteenth-century Nyingma master Mipham Rinpoche that every time he prayed to him, he believed he was in the presence of Manjushri. At fourteen, he joined Drakzong Monastery in Nyarong and took novice ordination with Khenpo Sönam Rinchen. In just one year, he managed to study countless sutras and tantras and had strong faith in the Great Perfection (Dzokchen) teachings, the highest teachings of the Nyingma school. Still only fifteen, he prayed sincerely to Mipham Rinpoche, repeating his prayer *Direct Showing of the Nature of Mind* (*Sems ngo mdzub btsugs*) one million times. He in that way realized the enlightened nature of the Great Perfection, an experience he describes in his *Great Commentary on the "Direct Showing of the Nature of Mind" of the Great Perfection* (*Sems ngo mdzub btsugs kyi 'grel ba man ngag gter gyi mdzod khang*).

In 1980, Jigme Phuntsok Rinpoche determined that it was time to set up an institute for the advanced learning and practice of the Buddhist teachings. In October of that year he founded the Larung Gar Buddhist Institute in Serthar. This institute, which includes facilities for monks, nuns, and laypeople alike, quickly became a major center of learning. In the twenty years following, Jigme Phuntsok Rinpoche taught and incorporated into the institute's curriculum all the Buddhist doctrines, including the five great treatises, profound tantric practices, pith instructions, commentaries, and tantras of the highest Great Perfection. He and the institute taught all of the four Tibetan Buddhist schools and traditions without bias. Several hundred khenpos and tulkus completed this extensive training and are now teaching in China, the Tibetan plateau, and other countries, bringing the great wisdom and knowledge of Jigme Phuntsok Rinpoche and the Buddha's vast teachings to hundreds of thousands of people. For this reason, this loving and wise teacher is revered as the most supreme guru in the Land of Snow.

So that others might also develop great faith in him, here is a short praise summarizing his nature and qualities.

Praise to the Dharma King Jigme Phuntsok Rinpoche

Prophesied by Buddha Shakyamuni and Great Padmasambhava
    many hundreds of years ago,
our loving Guru is the collective embodiment of the buddhas
    of the three times.
The manifestation of many Indian and Tibetan mahasiddhas,
the supreme being who obtains the fruit of a bodhisattva in this
    very lifetime,
the great master who is proficient in the ocean of sutras and
    tantras,
the supreme guardian of discipline who strictly maintains
    the precepts of the three vehicles,
the one who has perfected wisdom and compassion and is able
    to teach, debate, and compose with ease,
the tower of strength reviving Buddhism,
the Dharma general who propagates both sutras and tantras
    without bias,
the cooling moon that diminishes the discomfort and negativity
    of sentient beings,
the king who, like a wish-fulfilling jewel, liberates any being
    that sees, hears, touches, or thinks of him,
the perfect guide who leads sentient beings to Sukhavati,
    the Land of Bliss,
the current lineage holder of the Great Perfection,
the guru of all sentient beings at the time of degeneration,
and the brilliant sun that eradicates the darkness of the five
    degenerations.

ABOUT THE AUTHOR

Khenpo Yeshe Phuntsok was born in China's Sichuan province in 1971 and educated in both Chinese and Tibetan. In 1985, he entered Larung Gar Buddhist Institute, modern Tibet's most dynamic and fastest-growing Buddhist academy, to study with its renowned founder, Jigme Phuntsok Rinpoche. In 1988, he became a *khenpo*, a senior teacher, and was assigned to teach Rinpoche's Chinese students in 1996. This is his first book in English.

ABOUT WISDOM PUBLICATIONS

Wisdom Publications is the leading publisher of classic and contemporary Buddhist books and practical works on mindfulness. Publishing books from all major Buddhist traditions, Wisdom is a nonprofit charitable organization dedicated to cultivating Buddhist voices the world over, advancing critical scholarship, and preserving and sharing Buddhist literary culture.

To learn more about us or to explore our other books, please visit our website at www.wisdompubs.org. You can subscribe to our eNewsletter, request a print catalog, and find out how you can help support Wisdom's mission either online or by writing to:

Wisdom Publications
199 Elm Street
Somerville, Massachusetts 02144 USA

You can also contact us at 617-776-7416 or info@wisdompubs.org.

Wisdom is a 501(c)(3) organization, and donations in support of our mission are tax deductible.

Wisdom Publications is affiliated with the Foundation for the Preservation of the Mahayana Tradition (FPMT).

Creation and Completion
Essential Points of Tantric Meditation
Jamgön Kongtrül
Translated and introduced by Sarah Harding
Commentary by Khenchen Thrangu Rinpoche
176 pages | $16.95 | ebook $12.35

"Creation and completion meditation is the cornerstone of tantric Buddhist practice and draws upon a rich array of techniques and presumptions relating to moral cultivation. This book will be of great interest to both scholars and practitioners of Tibetan Buddhism."
—Janet Gyatso, Hershey Chair of Buddhist Studies, Harvard University

Becoming Vajrasattva
The Tantric Path of Purification
Lama Thubten Yeshe, Nick Ribush
Foreword by Lama Zopa Rinpoche
320 pages | $18.95 | ebook $13.81

"One of the great teachers of our time."
—Sogyal Rinpoche, author of *The Tibetan Book of Living and Dying*

To Dispel the Misery of the World
Whispered Teachings of the Bodhisattvas
Ga Rabjampa, Rigpa Translations
Foreword by Khenpo Appey
224 pages | $16.95 | ebook $12.35

"The marvelous commentary is translated so eloquently. This little book is a real gem."
—Cyrus Stearns, author of *Hermit of Go Cliffs*

Losing the Clouds, Gaining the Sky
Buddhism and the Natural Mind
Doris Wolter
320 pages | ebook $18.95

"An eclectic collection of writings on Dzogchen. Includes seven pieces by Sogyal Rinpoche. The many voices gathered here demonstrate the wide range of styles with which individual teachers of the past century have expressed the Great Perfection."
—*Buddhadharma*

Medicine and Compassion
A Tibetan Lama's Guidance for Caregivers
Chökyi Nyima Rinpoche, David R. Shlim
Foreword by Harvey Fineberg and Donald Fineberg
208 pages | $17.95 | ebook $10.89

"I was dumbfounded by how much Chokyi Nyima Rinpoche comprehends the emotional challenges facing doctors in relationship to their patients. He nails it time and time again. Magnificent! I shall continue to reread it just for the pleasure of the teachings, for the clarity of his mind, and for the purity of his heart. This is a very worthy project."
—Jon Kabat-Zinn, MD, author of *Full Catastrophe Living*